STRATEGY OF PEACE

WORLD PEACE FOUNDATION

40 Mt. Vernon Street, Boston, Massachusetts

Founded in 1910

THE World Peace Foundation is a non-profit organization which was founded in 1910 by Edwin Ginn, the educational publisher, for the purpose of promoting peace, justice and good-will among nations. For many years the Foundation has sought to increase public understanding of international problems by an objective presentation of the facts of international relations. This purpose is accomplished principally through its publications and by the maintenance of a Reference Service which furnishes on request information on current international problems. Recently increased attention has been focused on American foreign relations by study groups organized for the consideration of actual problems of policy.

STRATEGY OF PEACE

By

HENRY M. WRISTON
President, Brown University

WORLD PEACE FOUNDATION
Boston
1944

PREFACE

In this volume, President Wriston considers the broad strategy which the United States should follow in order to attain the general purposes of its participation in the war. We recognize the need of a sound strategy for the successful prosecution of the war. This book assumes that a sound strategy for the winning of the peace is just as necessary.

In Part I, the author offers a new approach to the relation of war to peace. He suggests that the distinctions which we commonly make are often misleading, and that in reality it is not so much a case of "either or" as of "more or less." Whether the relations between states appear to be peaceful and cooperative or hostile and antagonistic depends upon the manner in which certain basic elements, such as reason, culture, emotion, economic activity and force are employed.

Against this general background, President Wriston considers the position of the United States in terms of interests and commitments. He finds in our past record grounds for considerable satisfaction, though not for complacency; the explanation of many of the criticisms this past record is receiving and of the doubts that are currently expressed he finds in the "momentary mood of those who forget that we are dealing with forces in time as well as in space." His emphasis is on proper perspective and his whole endeavor is to show the need of seeing things in the large without giving undue emphasis to those values and considerations

v

which naturally greatly influence our thinking in time of war.

In his concluding part, President Wriston faces up to the problem which we will have to face sooner or later of making peace with the defeated powers. He considers the difficulties which arise from the fact that we are allied with others in this war, and the other difficulties which are the product of our constitutional system. He discusses in some detail the provisions of a proposed peace treaty which will at one and the same time provide a basis for agreement with our allies, lay the foundation for post-war international organization and have the best chance of being accepted by the United States Senate.

This work is presented as a stimulating contribution to the current public discussion of the problems of the peace, a discussion which it is hoped will lead to a better understanding of these problems as they present themselves and to wiser political action than after the last war.

LELAND M. GOODRICH
Director

July 18, 1944

CONTENTS

PART I
WAR AND PEACE

CHAPTER I

THE CENTRAL ISSUE

THE outstanding fact in the international relations of the world is the tragedy of war twice within a single generation. It is significant that the First World War, as it is now called, occurred after two great world peace conferences, and after the principles of international law, the mutual interests of nations, and the mobilization of public opinion had made war seem practically impossible to most people. The Second World War occurred after "a war to end war," after the organization of a League of Nations and a World Court, and after doctrines of political pacifism, as distinguished from religious pacifism, had gained wide acceptance. It started shortly after one leading statesman had declared that "we do not need to take up arms; . . . we can carry on a national war for the cause of humanity without shedding blood," and another had predicted peace in our time. It is evident that men with the most complete organizations available to give them information did not accurately assess the several events by which war came.

It is equally clear that there is no real consensus as to when the war actually began or when or how it will end. The United States is at war. From that assertion there could be no dissent. But if the question is asked, "When was the nation at peace?" some would answer, "Until December 7, 1941," others would cite the passage of the Lend-Lease Act, others the exchange of destroyers for bases, and

3

others would give still different answers. The varying dates would cover a considerable span of time. In the same way if one were to ask about the end of the war, some would make it synonymous with military victory, others with the signature of a treaty, and still others would put it far in the future beyond those formal episodes. Obviously great confusion exists as to both the beginning of the war and its conclusion, and there is urgent need to clarify our minds. Otherwise the war may be won and the peace lost—as has happened many times before in history.

In order to meet that vital issue it is necessary to understand what we mean by "peace" and what by "war," and how the transition is made from one to the other.

CHAPTER II

TOTAL WAR

MUCH thinking about this war is dominated by a German phrase which has been picked up and employed without adequate analysis. Men constantly talk and write about "total war." So general is the adoption of the catch phrase that any challenge to its accuracy is regarded with suspicion. Nevertheless, the words are deceptive, for in point of fact we do not have total war in America or anything remotely approaching it. Though they come closer to it in Germany, they do not have it even there.

The phrase is doubly misleading when used in America because it belongs to a system of ideas hostile to our own. Ludendorff summarized the point briefly: "War is the highest expression of the racial will to life, and politics must be subservient to conduct of war." "Politics—even in time of peace—must become totalitarian in anticipation of the life struggle between peoples." Total war, as a concept, is part of the fundamental scheme of the totalitarian state. "The nature of the total war determines the nature and form of the totalitarian state." "War is the essence of everything." It is possible, even as an idea, only where the state is the end and the individual the means.

The ideal of total war is a constituent element within a distinctive philosophy of life; it is part of the structure of political thought which assumes that war is not only *a* normal activity but *the* normal, and indeed the highest type of activity. "Germany's full virtue and beauty unfold only

5

in wartime." Under this political philosophy peace is desirable solely as preparation for war, and war—rather than peace—is an end in itself. The totalitarian regimes, it has well been said, "are governments at war, originating in war, aiming at war, thriving on war." They do not deny the fact. "War," said Robert Ley, Nazi Labor Front leader, "is the blessing of God. . . . In this war lies the rebirth of our nation." "War and courage," Nietzsche wrote, "have done more things than charity."

We can never really understand the present struggle without a complete and acute realization that we are fighting both a strong nation and a stubborn idea. Nazism claims to be a new order but some of its root concepts are very old. Certainly the notion that total war, as an ideal, is a recent development in thought is utterly false. The essence of total war has always existed whenever and wherever the soldier alone is a citizen; it was characteristic of the Middle Ages when the words "free men" meant "soldiers." If a man did not bear arms, he was not a free man. The Nazi philosophy of total war merely tricks out that ancient concept in modern verbal garb.

The democratic faith, on the contrary, regards peace as the normal and the highest activity of man, and war as a manifestation of failure to maintain life at its noblest and best level. We believe that the individual is the end and that the state exists as a means to serve him. Between these contrasting views of life there can be no compromise; we are dealing with antithetical absolutes; one must survive and the other must perish.

This consideration is vital, for if the philosophy and the substance of total war really represent truth, there can be no genuine peace. All the human longing to beat swords into ploughshares, so often referred to in Scripture and in secular literature, would represent mere self-deception. If the phrase "total war" were to be taken in its full and literal sense, not only the fact, but even the ideal, of peace would cease to exist. We should have to accept Nietzsche's passionate assertion: "Ye shall love peace as a means to new wars—and the short peace more than the long. . . . Ye say, a good cause will hallow even war? I say unto you, a good war hallows every cause." In the American system of ideas, on the other hand, war is a brief and violent physical means to quite different political ends. There must be room outside its false totality, consequently, for the major idea. Otherwise we are forced to adopt the Nazi concept of war as the normal state and peace as only an abnormal interlude.

The assumption that the current war is in fact and reality total, that it employs all our energies, is obviously wrong. There are vital forces quite outside the war. Many individuals pursue their normal occupations, and many more their regular avocations and recreations. Fashions and amusements, for example, still have a place in life. Theaters and dance halls are thronged even in the midst of bombings; race tracks draw record crowds even where manpower is shortest. In the same way large national energies are not wholly absorbed by the war. The discussion of the Beveridge Plan in Britain, the effort to achieve security "from the cradle to the grave," is far more relevant to time of peace than to war-time. In America there are many evidences of politics as usual. The idea that the war engrosses all thought and energy even in Germany is a fantastic misconception.

The phrase "total war" further confuses our thinking because it is employed to distinguish this war from previous struggles. It is assumed that never before have nations been so completely mobilized nor their energies so fully utilized. One has only to read the Decree of the Convention on August 23, 1793, during the French Revolution, to see how the entire populace was involved in that war:

"All citizens must discharge their debt to liberty. Some will give their labor, others their wealth, some their counsel, others their strength; all will give it the blood that flows in their veins. Thus all Frenchmen, all sexes, all ages are called . . . to defend liberty." "From this moment until . . . the enemies shall have been driven from the territory of the Republic, all citizens of France are in permanent requisition for the service of the armies. The young men will go forth to battle; the married men will make arms and transport food; the women will make tents, uniforms, and will serve in the hospitals; the children will prepare lint from old linen; the old men will gather in the public places to rouse the courage of the warriors, to excite hatred of kings and preach the unity of the Republic. National houses will be converted into barracks, public squares into factories of arms, and the earth of cellars will be examined to extract the saltpetre from it. Saddle horses will be requisitioned to complete the corps of cavalry; draught horses, other than those employed in agriculture, will be used for artillery and transport. The Committee of Public Safety is . . . authorized to set up all the buildings, factories and workshops which shall be considered necessary for the execution of this work, and to requisition for that object, in the whole extent of the Republic, the craftsmen and workers who can contribute to success."

If one compares that Decree with our present Selective Service Law, the relevant executive orders, and the regulations of the War Manpower Commission, it becomes clear that there was, perhaps, a closer approach to total mobilization in 1793 than 150 years later.

It is also assumed when this phrase is used that civilians are in more danger and are more harshly treated today than in earlier wars. We think of the bombing of cities and the consequent violation of immunities normally enjoyed by civilians as relatively new developments. In their present form they are partly new, but the bombardment, siege, and sack of cities, the robbery, abuse, enslavement, and slaughter of civilians are historical facts too often forgotten. The reality is that the "normal" immunities of civilians are the new idea. The period in which the rights of neutral states won recognition, when efforts were made to quarantine war and to extend the privileges of civilians came to its apogee with the Hague Peace Conferences. The era when those limitations upon the ravages of war were actually effective was, in the long perspective of history, very brief indeed. That we have taken them so much for granted is an illustration of how short is man's memory; immunity has a far briefer history than outrage.

"Total war" is further misleading because it implies that this war is "global" in a new sense. The difference is only one of degree, and not nearly so great as most people suppose. Few nations participating in the present struggle were not involved in the last war. Even in the eighteenth century there must have been something like global war when fighting was going on simultaneously in Europe, in North America, in the West Indies, and in India.

The so-called new interdependence of the world consists merely of modern evidences of an old phenomenon. It is true that the airplane and other recent developments have reduced the time of communication and lessened the significance of space, but the importance of these unquestioned facts has been overestimated. It is a common human weakness to overemphasize new factors and unduly discount old ones; novelty attracts attention and surface changes conceal more profound aspects of stability. We have been so overawed by speed in moving from place to place that we tend to forget the vital matter is what we do on arrival. Speed in achieving something trivial is not really earth shaking. In our time we have been so impressed with technological marvels that we have attributed to them significance far in excess of their genuine importance, great as that undoubtedly is. It remains a fact that Hitler was unable to ferry an army across the twenty-one mile Channel and invade Britain, just as were Napoleon and the Spaniards and the French in earlier days. Preparation to invade Europe from England absorbed enormous energies even with dominance on the sea and in the sky.

The reality of world interdependence, the substance of the "one world" concept, is very old. Nothing but the combination of modern arrogance and ignorance can make its recent manifestations appear like something new in kind rather than merely a change in degree. We may well remind ourselves that the Crusades to recover the Holy Places were an illustration of religious interdependence. The Holy Land, then, as now, was a land of Jews, Christians, and Moslems. The Moslems became dominant and the fact that Jerusalem was in the hands of the Saracens was most disturbing to Christendom. King Richard the Lion-Hearted, of England, tilted against the Saracens a good part of his reign, spending less than a year at home.

There was trade interdependence, too. Even the discovery of America was an accidental incident of the close interdependence of the East and the West. For many years Portuguese, Spaniards, and Englishmen sought new and shorter spice routes because spice was an essential, as the earlier counterpart of modern refrigeration. The complementary relationship of East and West long ago offered full proof of world solidarity.

Another illustration which preceded the development of "modern" transportation and communication is the opening of Japan in the middle of the nineteenth century. Many people regret that action, feeling that it opened Pandora's box, but it was inevitable. If Commodore Perry acting for America had not been the instrument, someone else acting for another country would have performed the service because the isolation of one nation was even then intolerable. Perry thus summarized the situation: "The Japanese . . . have no right, in the present condition of the world, to isolate themselves." Our action involved nothing of imperialism; his instructions were sincere in the statement: "This Government . . . does not seek . . . any exclusive commercial advantage for itself, but on the contrary desires and expects that whatever benefits may result . . . will ultimately be shared by the civilized world." There was no trace of aggrandizement or aggression. It was a dramatic incident demonstrating how compact was the world in the days before the cable, the radio, the airplane, and the modern dreadnought.

The general and uncritical employment of the expression "total war" is a barrier to understanding the struggle in which we are engaged. From whatever point of view we approach the phrase, its dangers are clear. It lumps together different ideas and gives a false appearance of coherence and truth to them all. When employed as a description of our national mobilization, it is so inexact as to be seriously misleading in its sweeping claim; when used to distinguish this war from earlier ones, its validity is limited. But the careless assumption to the contrary has concealed its deadly quality as an expression of a political philosophy antithetical to our own. In that vital aspect it has a long historical background which has been largely overlooked because of current concentration upon an intense modern exemplar. Minds fixed on Hitler ought to recall that he is only a contemporary and transient embodiment of an ideal and a program in absolute opposition to ours.

Realization of that fact makes it obvious that we must defeat the idea of total war as well as its protagonists. We must achieve a lasting moral and intellectual, in addition to an immediate political and military, victory. In the last war we failed at that point. Much emphasis was laid upon hanging the Kaiser, as in this war great stress is placed upon punishing war criminals. The Kaiser was not hung. Instead he was allowed to work out his years of futility on the wood pile. By that process, it was clearly demonstrated he was not essential to the system of ideas to which he merely gave public expression. Though he was powerless in exile, the doctrines, never extirpated, continued to influence German thought. A prediction made by Thomas Mann in 1914 came true: he called for German victory, and said that if defeat came instead, "Europe would never be safe from Germany's militarism." The fall of the Kaiser, who personified militarism, left the idea unscathed. The branch was lopped off, but the root was not destroyed. Hanging Wilhelm II would have given many people personal satisfaction, yet that alone would have done nothing to destroy the political philosophy he represented. The Kaiser was banished, just as Napoleon was immured on St. Helena; in neither instance was Caesarism effectively scotched.

The emphasis upon punishing individuals this time must not withdraw attention from the fact that they are only the symbols, not the substance, of the trouble. The real menace is the system of ideas. If Hitler goes back to paper hanging, it will be similar to the Kaiser going on with his wood chopping—a demonstration of the futility of an individual who no longer effectively represents dominant concepts. Hitler's personal fate, like that of Napoleon and the Kaiser before him, is relatively unimportant; it is far more vital that the doctrines which he has sponsored be overthrown. That involves the defeat of the *concept* of total war. The whole totalitarian structure must be destroyed in all its manifestations. It must be overwhelmed not merely physically but intellectually. Physical victory without moral supremacy would be sterile.

CHAPTER III

THE DISTINCTION BETWEEN WAR AND PEACE

THE definition of war and peace may be approached from three different points of view. The first is deceptively clear, the second is significantly vague, and the third becomes clear only in perspective.

First, there is the legal aspect of the difference between war and peace. This is deceptively clear. In December 1941 Japan attacked the United States and declared war upon this country and Great Britain, and immediately thereafter Germany and Italy declared war upon the United States. In each case the United States reciprocated. The joint resolution declaring war upon Japan was adopted by Congress on the 8th of December and was signed by the President at 4:10 P.M. Eastern War Time. Under the Constitution of the United States, that was, for the American people, the legal change to war in place of peace. But by the time that signature became effective, every United States battleship based upon Pearl Harbor was already out of action. The legal inception of war did not correspond with the moment of war's physical impact, much less with its substantive reality. Yet that definite day, December 8, 1941, will be set down in all the books of history as the date for America's entry into the war. It corresponds with the legal status, but with no other; that is why, though it is clear, it is nonetheless deceptive.

14

Similarly, there will come a time when a treaty of peace will be signed, its ratification will be consented to by the Senate, ratifications will be exchanged by the State Department, and the President will proclaim it. From the legal point of view that will be the moment of peace. Among those who read these words probably not one can remember exactly when that event took place at the end of the last war. The date of the Armistice is familiar, the time of the signature of the Treaty of Versailles is fairly well known, but the Senate did not consent to its ratification and the American treaty with Germany was not proclaimed until November 14, 1921.

The legal distinction between war and peace is not without significance; property rights and many other interests are modified by it. But relative to the total pattern of life as affected by war, this excessively precise legal distinction is vastly less important than the political aspect.

By contrast, the political distinction between war and peace is significantly vague. People talk about the "white" war which preceded the "red" war. They refer to the economic war which preceded the battles. They speak of the "long armistice" between the Treaty of Versailles and the outbreak of this war, as though there never was an interval of genuine peace. Some regard the present war as beginning in 1931 at the time of the Manchurian incident and the development of the Stimson Doctrine. Others say war began in 1934 when Japan denounced the Washington treaties. Still others think it started in 1935 when Italy attacked Ethiopia and defeated the concept of sanctions. Others would connect it with the German occupation of the Rhineland in 1936. Every person has his favorite time, some suggesting the civil war in Spain, others the *Anschluss*, yet

15

others the Sudeten crisis. Each of those claims has a plausible basis. It is obvious that every act of aggression was part of a maturing crisis; the declaration of war is only a culminating step which completes the development.

Defining the state of war politically, therefore, is like inquiring when some functional disorder took on serious pathological qualities. It may start as some mild or benign affliction, but slowly or swiftly by unperceived degrees develop to a point where it menaces life itself. At what moment in that tragic sequence did the disease begin?

Peace comes politically in the same way as war itself. The peace treaty, whatever its legal effects, will not ensure political peace. Genuine peace, if it is ever achieved, will come through many channels over many long years. It will be a wise man indeed who can set a precise date upon which others, equally well informed, will agree.

The third distinction between war and peace is military; it is clear only in long perspective. This is called a global war, and many insist it is one war. But common sense makes it obvious that so long as the Soviet Union is not at war with Japan or the United States with Finland, the statement that there is a single war is imprecise.

The same difficulty appears when the chronology of the war is examined. The use of force began with the Manchurian incident in 1931. The current phase of the war in China began in 1937. Fighting took place in Africa in 1935 with the conquest of Ethiopia, and on the continent of Europe with the occupation of Albania in the spring of 1939. In the period since the declaration of war by Great Britain against Germany on September 3, 1939, some thirty-five other nations have declared war and others have severed diplomatic relations with the Axis. Denmark and Norway, Belgium and the Netherlands, Italy, the Balkan States, the Soviet Union, Finland, Japan and the United States all became involved in the fighting at different times.

Everybody knows that the war did not begin everywhere at once. The German tactics were to divide and conquer—divide politically, economically, and in a military sense. Neither can the war end in all parts of the world simultaneously. That fact shapes military planning. Allied strategy undertakes one major enterprise at a time. As Germany sought to subdue a single nation or a small group of nations in turn, so the Allies do not wage war on all fronts with equal resources and energy in the expectation of achieving total victory in all theaters at once. The anticipation is that other of the satellite nations in addition to Italy may well drop out before Germany is fully beaten, and the grand strategy has anticipated the destruction of German military power before the Japanese are finally whipped.

Such military facts are characteristic of all war. The Hundred Years' War between France and Britain was by no means a period of uninterrupted fighting; the name could be applied to the era only in retrospect. Similarly, the Napoleonic wars were interrupted by truces, by reversal of alliances, and by treaties of peace which proved temporary. Yet in the long perspective the whole period had a certain unity; the successive phases of the lengthy series of struggles are now regarded as constituting one war. Those are illustrations of what is meant by the assertion that the military aspects of war and peace are comprehensible only in perspective.

War is a legal, political, and military fact; its appearance is different when observed from those various points of view. Since the distinction between peace and war is

17

legally clear, politically vague, and militarily plain only in perspective, the effort to roll all three types of description into one has resulted in confusion of thought. The need is to find a different mode of approach. Some common denominator must harmonize these conflicting bases of judgment. To discover it, we must look at elements common to both peace and war.

CHAPTER IV

ELEMENTS OF WAR AND PEACE

THERE are many common elements in war and peace; that must inevitably be true since the fabric of life is seamless. Five, however, call for discussion in connection with the basic problems of international relations—reason, culture, emotion, economic activity, and force. All are present in time of peace, and all are present in time of war. This being so, war and peace cannot be mutually exclusive terms. Instead, they must be relative terms; as there is no such thing as total war, so also the world has never known absolute peace. The difference between war and peace consists in a shift of emphasis within and among these five elements. The transition from one to the other is marked by crises, such as a declaration of war or a treaty of peace, but those crises, though important, are more dramatic than significant. They often consist largely in the recognition of realities which already exist. They are like milestones by a road; they do not advance the traveler, but they indicate how far he has gone.

Those who, prior to 1939, felt there was no war because blood had not been shed obviously missed the point. Similarly those who now demand that we "get on with the war," forgetting the peace till after victory, also miss the point. As every act of aggression helped produce war, so every event of the war affects the peace. The great German commentator on war, Clausewitz, called war "nothing but a continuation of political activities with other means

19

intermingled." That is certainly true. Those who expect first to win the war and subsequently to make the peace are not viewing the problem realistically. The reconquest of Ethiopia—already half forgotten in the rush of events—affected the peace; the fact that the United States has not declared war on Finland and that the Soviet Union has not declared war on Japan affects the peace; the decision to invade North Africa first rather than make a direct assault on Europe, completely altering the status of France and the standing of the people with whom the Allies dealt in North Africa, affected the peace; and the assassination of Darlan was influential not only for the conduct of the war but for the peace as well.

There has been a good deal of discussion of "stages" in peacemaking. Such stages are artificial, not to say unreal. It has been proposed, for example, that one important stage would be a kind of halt to give time for men to rethink their problems and let their passions cool. It is urged that the fury of war does not constitute a good mood for devising a successful peace. That is unfortunately true, but experience shows it may be the lesser of two evils. The hoped for cooling-off period before the "final" peace may work in reverse. Delay is likely to result in heating up.

That is what occurred after the last war. The settlement of the reparations question was postponed, in order, as Prime Minister Lloyd George said, to allow passions to cool before the final sum was fixed. If that was the purpose, the reality proved quite different. The claims became larger as time passed; anger mounted even higher than the figures. After the last war, also, the determination of a number of boundary disputes was delayed in order to settle them by plebiscite under the principle of self-determination. In several instances the waiting period did not allay passion; on the contrary it provided time for the incubation of hates. Human nature is so constituted that postponement of an issue, delay in reaching a decision, can work in either direction, or even in both directions at once—cooling off in one respect and heating up in another. That is a common experience; we all know men with hot heads and cold feet.

The actual fact is that war and peace are two parts of a larger entity and they must be made together. There is no other conceivable way. Clarity of thinking, therefore, requires us to blunt the sharp edges of those two words which have been given a false precision. Peace and war, if we regard them as mutually exclusive, confuse the war effort and bedevil the making of peace.

The most revealing way to approach the problem is to consider war and peace as phases of national policy. That is the thread through the maze. National policy is continuous, but it constantly changes in direction, intensity, and relative emphasis. In the pursuit of the objectives of national policy statesmen select different means among its various resources and employ them positively or negatively, constructively or destructively. When the emphasis upon the positive and constructive means is strongest, we have what is called peace; when negative or destructive action is dominant, we have what is called war. This being so, we may apply a practical test to determine whether a policy leads to war or peace. If it is negative, it is hostile to peace; if it is constructive, it is leading away from war.

The manner in which national policy brings peace or war may be expressed in other terms; a choice is made between economical or extravagant methods. The five elements common to peace and war can be arranged roughly in order of cost in money and goods, in effort and life. Starting with the most economical and moving to the most extravagant, they can be set down in approximate order— reason, culture, emotion, economic activity, force. Reason costs nothing but mental effort; force costs everything, even life itself. When the emphasis is upon reason and culture, national policy is employing the most economical means, and the tendency is toward peace. When the dominant emphasis is put upon force, the same ends are sought by an extravagant method and we have war. The objectives of war and peace are the same, namely the accomplishment of national policy. The means employed are also the same— the five elements. One difference between war and peace lies in the economy or the extravagance with which the implements of policy are selected and employed. Economy and extravagance are relative; this reminds us again that war and peace are not absolute terms.

Stating the problem in this manner—positive versus negative, economical versus extravagant—simplifies the issue somewhat. At best, it can never be really simple, for the shift of emphasis within and among the five elements is continuous and fluid, and there are currents, great or small, which cut across the main stream of events. A country will often, indeed usually, pursue mutually contradictory policies at the same time. Some of the eddies go round and round even as they move down—or up—the main stream, creating a confused surface above a steady drift, which, itself, changes pace in different circumstances. So, for example, in the United States lend-lease and neutrality were simultaneous but inconsistent elements in our national program. If one were to follow the incoherencies of political, economic, and social thought and action, it would be evident that, whereas we think in terms of the stream of events, the flow is immensely complicated.

Indeed, it is essential to emphasize that national policy is never wholly clear or perfectly consistent. It is so vast in its reach and its problems are so complex and must involve the participation of so many people that perfect teamwork is impossible. Moreover policy and particularly the specific practices designed to effectuate it are always the result of compromise. In recent years it has been commonly asserted that dictators do not have to compromise. One of the alleged "virtues" of dictatorships, often put forward, is that they can arrive at decisions more readily, and pursue them more consistently. The dictators, it is said, are free from the necessity of making the concessions which public opinion, with its confusion and contradictions, forces upon a democracy. This is specious reasoning, based upon untrue assumptions. Even if everything were left to the dictator, national policy would still not be consistent, for no individual is completely so, and the dictators have notoriously been men of moods and passions which made them peculiarly inconsistent in thought and policy.

Practically, however, the dictator does not have a free hand; he is dependent on a bureaucracy. In a very important sense, the more absolute his power is supposed to be, the more dependent he is in practice. His function is often to work out a compromise between the competing views of the leading officials of the bureaucratic structure. The more he appears to be dominant, the more he is likely to be dominated by the bureaucracy. And bureaucracy is never consistent; it sprawls too much; its officials are too jealous, too ambitious, too tenacious of their vested interests. Its fatal defect is lack of coordination, and no organizing genius has ever yet been found who could supply that essential element. It is a fallacy to expect more consistency in a dictatorship than a democracy.

National policy in any type of government, therefore, is inconsistent to a greater or lesser degree. In America, even during war-time, we observe simultaneously an acute shortage of manpower and gross wastes of manpower. During war we keep some practices proper only in peace, but alter others to facilitate the use of force.

If national policy is not coherent, it may happen—and in practice it occurs continually—that part makes for peace and part for war. Under such circumstances war and peace are of necessity relative, not absolute, terms. To emphasize still further the relativity of war and peace, it must be remembered that all countries pursue national policies which utilize the same essential elements. Each program of each nation has not only its characteristic bent but its own particular confusions, incoherencies, and contradictions.

The sum total of all these national policies of all the countries comprises the international policies which produce war or peace. Thus there are not only tensions within a nation. There are also strains between nations and groups of nations. Even among allies differences of policy have often been severe enough to produce a rupture; that is why there have been many historic reversals of alliance. Such consequences would be more frequent but for the fact that even greater enemy pressures force the allies together. That is the reason the problems of peace are never limited merely to a settlement with the enemy even when the foe is overthrown. The postponed issues and accumulated irritations between the allies themselves urgently demand action. Peace has been lost almost as often by quarreling among victorious allies as by failure to deal adequately and wisely with the defeated enemy.

These many complicated factors suggest that simple explanations of how nations go to war should be viewed with great skepticism. There was a time when it was fashionable to blame "the armament makers," assigning them the principal responsibility for war. Without question, some of them did exercise malign influences. They are not to be defended, but it hides the truth to load the blame upon them exclusively; they were only one influence among many. At another time the international bankers, at another big business, at another ambitious politicians, at another public hysteria were held responsible. All these, and many others, have been put forward as "the key." In one way or another, all have contributed to bringing on the ultimate tragedy of war, but there are thousands of other influences.

The explanation of the coming of war, therefore, is never simple. That fact should suggest to our minds that the achievement of peace cannot be a simple matter either. It does not consist of "abolishing this" and "organizing that." By itself a world parliament might not be an instrument of peace. It might make confusion even more confounded; it might prove to be a Tower of Babel. An international police force might protect the peace, but it might stimulate war. A world army might be ruled by a clique of colonels and bring the kind of difficulties that we have seen in Poland, in Argentina, and elsewhere. An army protects peace only so long as the army itself is controlled.

Since there is no simple solution, we come back to the realization that the problem of war and peace is mastered only by the continuous, wise, and constructive employment of the elements common to both.

CHAPTER V

REASON

REASON is the basic element in international relations. It is by far the least expensive; its only cost is in mental effort. It is also the most flexible; it can yield to intelligent and informed criticism, and be reshaped through open-minded discussion. It is one of the two fundamental elements which has a fixed and consistent direction. Force is the other. But reason and force press toward opposite poles. Reason, properly defined, is always a positive element in any situation. Force, even under the most favorable environment, is always negative. Reason advances peace; force impairs it.

In the right environment reason is the most powerful instrument in the whole armory of policy. With proper leverage it exerts a much more effective and a far more permanent influence than force. Force may temporarily alter behavior, but a change of mind by the enlightened use of reason permanently redirects policy. Its employment makes possible a persuasive exposition of national policy both at home and abroad. The very effort to systematize policy, in order to expound it and meet rational criticism, encourages consistency. The imaginative use of reason also promotes insight into the policies of other nations and the supple adjustment of each to the other.

The international instrument of reason is diplomacy. National budgets show that usually the foreign office is

26

the least costly branch of the government. However valuable its results, talk is cheap. Yet, by the weight of reason and the power of insight and the influence of flexible argument, Talleyrand saved France from many of the normal consequences of the defeat of Napoleon. Reason and its fruits proved more potent than force. That is only one well-known historical illustration from an almost infinite number which could be cited. Diplomacy is not adequately appreciated. As Secretary Hull said, it "is not . . . a mysterious game carried on by diplomats . . . all over the world." It is the daily, continuous application of reason to the problems of international relationships. There is no substitute for it; none should be sought.

There is a feeling that however important reason may be under conditions of peace, it does not play a significant part during a war. We are often told that when fighting begins, nothing counts but force. On the contrary, reason exerts a vital influence even when the roar of battle is loudest. It is used to persuade hostile satellites of their error and so to detach adherents from the enemy; and it is employed to hold allies firmly together and draw new support into coalition. That accounts for the frequent visits of heads of states in war-time. The great conferences are familiar to all, but many forget the less spectacular meetings, which are nonetheless valuable. For example, President Roosevelt made a trip to Mexico in 1943. It furnished an opportunity for the employment of persuasion in a favorable environment. It had a marked effect upon the cooperation of the two nations in the war.

During war-time the public speeches of world figures are consciously designed to have an influence both at home and abroad, among friends and enemies. It is unchallenged historical fact that the addresses of President Wilson were influential in leading to peace overtures at the end of the last war. Peace feelers are continuously being made, directly or indirectly, by public or secret means; the play of reason is vital to those proposals.

The world has suffered two catastrophic wars in a single generation. One important explanation is that we have lived in an age when reason is no longer trusted as the dominant element in international relations. That is why we hear so much about "power politics," about "geopolitics," and other political "realities" which discount reason as a vital force.

It is difficult to realize how powerful and how widespread has been the revolt against reason in our time. If this is an age of revolution, as so often asserted, in no other aspect of life is the evidence of breaking away from long-accepted patterns so clear. Disbelief in the potency of reason as a decisive factor in historical development and in the determination of contemporary policy is widespread, and it is deep seated. In no other way can one explain the failure to see at an early date the inevitable consequences of the fascist program.

That discount upon the power and even the validity of reason is a fundamental cause of this war. One of the prophetic exponents of the "new age" declared:

"The fight against the age of reason which we are entering on, is a fight against liberalism all along the line. In the course of this fight we shall realize how brief an epoch the Age of Reason has been; . . . how ephemeral its legacy. . . . All great achievements [in Germany] were produced in the teeth of the age of reason." "All who were in any way creatively active realized that the nation's salvation did not lie in debating-

28

matches, and consequently held more and more aloof from parliaments. . . . Germany has proved too good for parliaments."

Oswald Spengler, whose writing had a great influence even in America, proclaimed a new era:

"The age old barbarism which for centuries lay bound and hidden under the severe discipline of a high culture is again awakening that warlike healthy joy in one's own strength, which despises the age of rationalistic thought and literature, that unbroken instinct of a strong race which wishes to live otherwise than under the pressure of a mass of books and bookish ideals."

Hitler never spoke of reason except with scorn; he asserted that "an unspoiled generation . . . will consciously return to the primitive instinct." He proclaimed his dependence upon intuition; he spoke of his inflexible will; he boasted that he thought with his blood. "Feeling," he said, "often decides more accurately than reason."

While Germany produced the most extravagant expressions, Italy was not far behind; fascism required the repudiation of reason as the principal guide to policy. Mussolini talked of discipline; his vast and searing contempt for democracy was predicated upon its rationalism. "My program," he declared, "is action, not thought." "To expect reason directly from the people and through the people is a chimera."

Japanese militarism, in like manner, involved a similar revolt against the rationalism upon which democracy depends. The Japanese people have been indoctrinated in blind loyalty to the Emperor. They are schooled to reject reason when it conflicts with imperial dogma. "For the Japanese," said Ludendorff, "service for the Emperor and thus for the State is prescribed by his experience of God. . . . In the unity of racial heritage and faith and in the philosophy of life erected upon them resides the strength of the Japanese people."

The significance of the repudiation of reason, the substitution of mysticism, discipline, and emotions in the nations at war with us cannot be overstated. They all closed the best channel of international intercourse.

The drift away from reason as a primary guide for action did not fail to influence the United States. Even our country whose Constitution begins "We the People," and whose Declaration of Independence is predicated upon "a decent respect to the opinions of mankind," felt the impact of this revolutionary force. We had a political movement called technocracy that planned to substitute technology for reason. It never captured public opinion but it was a symptom of a widespread influence. Moreover there were far more important, though less obvious and crass, manifestations of lack of faith in reason. The whole emphasis upon economic determinism, with its many ramifications in our national life, is clearly predicated upon the idea that material interests hobble reason.

Influential schools of sociologists and social psychologists laid great stress upon the assertion that most men do not act in logical fashion to achieve well-envisioned or well-defined ends. Subconscious and semiconscious "drives" were regarded as vastly more potent, "interests" of one kind or another were pictured as more compelling. Reason was discounted "scientifically." The vogue of Freud in this country is significant in that connection. Many years ago Thomas Mann spoke of Freud's work as "opposition to rationalism." The importance of the rage for behaviorism

30

as a discount upon reason has been too long overlooked.

The effect of anti-intellectualism upon education was notable. Learning was described as the formation of habits, the cultivation of standard responses to definite, controlled stimuli. Training in "skills," not the discipline of the mind through logical processes, was proposed as the central factor in the educational regime. In fact, the discipline of reason was ridiculed.

Illustrations of anti-intellectualism could be multiplied indefinitely. It is fair to say that skepticism regarding the primacy of reason has become at least as prevalent as religious skepticism. In such an atmosphere it is not to be wondered that the last twenty-five years have seen relatively minor contributions to philosophy and political theory. In such an intellectual climate passionate faith in democracy was certain to wither.

It is not surprising that an age in retreat from reason as its guide produced no figure of classic proportions in diplomacy. Doubt regarding the validity of reason made the path of diplomacy needlessly stony. It seemed incredible that men talking around a green baize table could be dealing with realities. Instead there was a strong tendency to measure commitments in terms of power rather than reasonableness. A balance sheet of physical assets and liabilities seemed more significant than a rational exposition of a deep and tenaciously held philosophy of world politics. Under those circumstances the most flexible as well as the most powerful instrument of policy was not fully exploited.

A return to passionate faith in reason would constitute an important step in winning the war and would prove even more vital in achieving a satisfactory and continuous peace. That is no simple, or short-run, proposal. It will require a revolution in philosophic outlook. The anti-intellectualism from which we now suffer was expounded in the closing decades of the nineteenth century. The loss of faith in the rational authority of intelligence began among intellectuals. Only slowly did the blight upon reason extend the area of its infection. The return to faith in reason cannot be achieved by facile gestures; no one can draw a blueprint for its accomplishment. It will require a profound intellectual reorientation which is always both difficult and slow.

When the Constitution of the United States was framed in 1787, reason was recognized as the dominant element in the formation and control of public policy. Faith in reason stimulated its employment, just as doubts concerning the efficiency of reason in our own day induced dependence upon economic leverage and resort to force. The records of the Convention which drew up the Constitution are available; in modern times there is no parallel to the group of men discussing political theory, the nature of the political structure, and the purposes of political life.

After the instrument was drafted, *The Federalist* papers, written by Hamilton, Jay, and Madison, made an appeal to the understanding of the common man. They were designed to give citizens a firm grasp upon the meaning of the Constitution. The arguments were not watered down for infantile minds. Faith in human reason protected the authors from confusing "untutored" with "incompetent"; they did not regard "reason directly from the people and through the people" as a "chimera." The writers expected readers to make an effort to follow their reasoning and they did not pander to mental laziness or moral lassitude.

The discussions which then took place, not only among those leaders, but among plain men in every town and hamlet, constituted one of the most remarkable instances of adult education in all history. The influence of that great debate was not merely temporary; it not only established the Constitution; it was also a vital factor in developing the unusual political competence displayed by the statesmen of the young republic. They framed their policies under the stimulus of a lively and intelligent public opinion.

The contrast with our own day, so far as confidence in reason is concerned, is suggested by the "modern" interpretation of the origins of the Constitution as the attempt of men who had speculated in government securities to make their investment good. Most recent historical studies of that decisive event in our political development have rested upon analyses of economic, social, or other "interests," and have grossly underemphasized the appeal of reason.

Reason is indispensable; neither force nor any other element in policy offers a substitute—force least of all. Even unconditional surrender will bring peace only if reason is properly employed as the primary instrument in the exploitation of victory. Blücher made a classic exclamation: "May the fruits reaped by the swords of the army not be destroyed by the pens of the ministers." They have been so destroyed again and again. It should be a reminder that there are no substitutes for wisdom and clear perception, for eternal vigilance and unwearied patience in the application of reason.

The substance of diplomacy should be precisely the process of logical analysis and of rational exposition applied to international affairs. It should be a quiet, faithful, consistent, continuous, and unhurried application of reason to the divergent aims and policies of the nations. The public aspects of diplomacy are vastly more significant than its secret consultations, for its purpose is to arrive as near a consensus as possible; it attempts to remove friction by insight and mutual concession. The more fully the people are kept informed of the major issues and the relevant arguments, the more temperate and stable—the more pacific—policy and action are certain to be.

CHAPTER VI

CULTURE

CULTURE is not often considered, in America, as an important factor in international relations. That is not surprising in a materialistic age, which tends to discount all intangibles. Geographical "realities," economic resources, the military potential are much more in the public mind—and in the minds of leaders, both scholarly and political.

Yet this neglected intangible has a vital reality; indeed it supplies one of the most stable foundations of policy; it is least subject to momentary influences and tricky manipulation. So deep are its roots and so strong its fabric that it can defy geography, economic forces, and military might. It is a fact of first importance, for example, that the Iberian Peninsula has an influence in Central and South America which cannot be explained on grounds of geographical propinquity, climatic similarity, economic interest, unity of race, and certainly not on the basis of genuine political interest. The bond is fundamentally a cultural tie; yet it is so significant that it has required vigorous and persistent effort upon the part of the United States to acquire a comparable influence.

That illustration calls attention to the fact that this element of policy tends to divide the world as well as to unite it; like most other factors it exerts both a positive and a negative attraction, and often simultaneously in different phases of action.

35

At its deepest and broadest we speak of culture in terms of "civilization"; it is composed of what we have learned intellectually, esthetically, morally in ages of living together on this planet. In all times and places men have wrestled with the same basic problems and have made varied responses which have, however, many and profound common characteristics. The memory and awareness of those common elements grow more conscious and pressing as the world is knit together. Appreciation of that fundamental commonalty is a powerful bond.

Superimposed upon this broad foundation are particularist manifestations. The culture of a nation represents the sum of the values it holds dear. It is its tradition as contrasted with its history; it is composed of those things which have survived as part of the public consciousness, which have come to be regarded as characteristic, as indigenous, and as precious. Every culture has distinctive elements which cannot be understood, much less appreciated, except with great difficulty. Contrasts in essential values, differences in esthetic and moral traditions, varieties of awareness, all these give unique qualities to culture. That is why throughout history foreigners have seemed to be "barbarians," "stranger" has usually meant "enemy." Differences of language are barriers not only to an appreciation of literature, but to an understanding of political, social, and economic ideas generally. Varieties of religious faith and practice have been violently divisive forces, although the religious impulse tends to unite mankind. Divergent traditions in the tonality of music and in esthetic standards in art often serve to make mutual understanding more difficult.

Whenever there is a clash between two concepts of

civilization, or any of its essential values, the difficulties of international relations are heightened. Sometimes the conflict is inherent, the result of long historical tradition. Such is the division between Orient and Occident which led to Kipling's famous, and oft regretted, aphorism, "Oh, East is East, and West is West, and never the twain shall meet." Beneath the grand unity of mankind are divisions which reflect many contrasts in tradition, value judgment, and taste. Only the most patient and persistent effort can bridge the gaps.

Cultural frictions are heightened unconsciously by nationalism, and may be still further stimulated as part of a calculated policy. When, therefore, a nation regards itself as a peculiar people or a master race or adopts any other myth which segregates it from the rest of mankind, it has a deep political significance for international relations. The "facts," the "hard realities" give way to a fiction, but one with powerful consequences. The most continuous and striking example is supplied by Germany. William II in a proclamation to his Eastern Army expressed the point with crude finality: "Remember that you are the chosen people." The same theme has been played with many variations by Hitler.

A chosen people would inevitably have a distinctive cultural ideal. Thomas Mann made that explicit point early in the last war. Germans, he wrote, "have never been as enamored of the word civilization as their western neighbors. . . . Germans have always preferred Kultur." He accepted "the fundamental antagonism . . . between Kultur and civilization" proclaimed by Nietzsche; indeed Mann wrote that "the concept of Kultur really occupied the central position in our own war-ideology." In that faith, the

37

Kaiser summoned his subjects "to take up the task of being God's instrument for the spreading of His Kultur." Hitler, following in the footsteps of his predecessor, promised a new order "founded upon the victorious sword of a ruling race bending the world to the service of a higher Kultur."

Such an outlook upon international relations rejects the bonds of civilization; it transcends, and so escapes, the trammels of common morality. The deified state creates its own ethic; the master race must have "an intellectual and a moral standard peculiar to itself." Book burning is natural to such a view. Hitler felt that civilization was the "enemy of true spiritual and living levels," and that in his fight for Germany's "existence," "all reflections concerning humanity or aesthetics resolve themselves to nothing and are excluded." Except for its consequences, such bombast would be a laughing matter. But the results of this *Kulturkampf* have been devastating.

We who are not German cannot readily grasp what the word "Kultur" means. It rejects the "cold rationalism" of Western civilization. As Thomas Mann explained, "There enters into the concept of Kultur an element of the wonderful and the mystical." It reflects something primitive; there is a communion, "an intimate union between themselves and the natural forces of the Universe whose action they intuitively apprehend." Kultur is to be understood "with the blood," and is expressed in feeling. It also involves "a human discipline designed to utilize" natural forces. To that end the military ideal dominates even scholarship. "The same discipline makes the soldier and the scholar efficient," declared Nietzsche. "That iron insistence accounts for the extraordinary degree of efficiency which is combined with intense emotionalism and

38

complete ethical unrestraint." Kultur accepts the brutality of nature without qualm; making no attempt to mitigate that quality, it adopts and exploits bestiality; therefore it does not shrink from force. Indeed mastery is part of the essential idea; it is the only "civilizing" influence in the modern world that anyone believes can really be spread by force.

This conscious, even strained and fantastic, distortion of history involves a reversal of human values. Harped upon, dogmatized, indoctrinated, endlessly repeated in a thousand variants, it laid the foundation early in the twentieth century for a war of cultures. Writing during the struggle, Mann designated it as "ultimately . . . the cause of the war." The Nazis later put their energies upon "the deliberate fanning of the flames of difference." It was a conscious effort at spiritual isolation as a prelude to the conquest of other cultures. We can properly call this new conflict a *Kulturkampf*, applying to it the name given Bismarck's opposition to the Latin, or Roman, tradition, in defense of pure Germanic ideals.

Those who are so preoccupied with geographic and economic "realities" that they overlook this source of the war and this problem of the peace are striving for a fruitless victory. Twice in one generation the German leaders have reminded us that culture can be an instrument of war as well as a bond of peace.

Hitler hates culture in the broad and catholic sense precisely because of its universality; he could never create the myth of a chosen people if they were an integral part of a universal life. He resents culture because it supplies a fundamental continuity in the grand outline of mankind's history. For example, the arts provide a treasury of knowledge and appreciation more completely a bond of union than was Latin to medieval scholars. Their language of beauty is as readily and perpetually available to foe as friend. It requires no translation and no interpreter. It is so fundamental and so nearly world wide that it defies censorship. Even though the picture or the sculpture cannot be seen, even though the music be stilled, and even though the book be burned, no censor can control the memory and no dictator can suborn the imagination.

Similarly there is a common treasury of literature, even when it must be read in translation. Its masterpieces have an appeal so universal in space, so perpetual in time, and so deeply imbedded in the emotional life of the world that they remain a valid humane reserve against current dislocations. The Bible, for instance, appears in over a thousand languages and dialects. It is a great historical record of the search for a spiritual interpretation of the universe, of the effort to discover a first cause among transient causes and an explanation of the meaning of life which is neither ephemeral nor distracted. Within that record are to be found all the stigmata of total war: annihilation, pestilence, bestiality, overwhelming grief, courage and faith, the triumph of the wrong and the victory of the right. There the whole range of human emotions, human weaknesses, human strengths are revealed, and with them an emerging insight into the mind of God and evidence that the moral order has powers of recovery beyond every human anticipation. All the greatest literature shares with the Bible this capacity to reflect the essential unity of mankind; it stresses our common heritage and supplies a bond stronger than the forces that divide men.

Intellectual comradeship is developed by the interchange

of ideas and artistic work, by the supranationalism of science and scholarship generally. The universities of the world have common origins, a like basic organization, an unbroken historic continuity, and traditions so deep and so strong that they overcome temporary dislocations. They are dynamic forces dedicated to the search for truth; that quest goes on continuously in science, in philosophy, and in esthetics. Intellectual cooperation is momentarily crippled in time of war but never wholly suspended. In the midst of strife the libraries of Europe and America make their plans to fill out, after the fighting, the missing publications in their long cultural interchange. Evidences of universality appear in the Oath of Hippocrates under which surgeons take as scrupulous care of prisoners of war as of their own men. Likewise, in spite of strife, efforts to control epidemics continue. Illustrations could be multiplied endlessly.

Culture, therefore, must not be underestimated. In fact this powerfully human aspect of life constitutes one of the most significant factors in international relations. It is no less vital because it is unobserved. Psychology has shown in recent years that some of the drives which strongly influence behavior are subconscious or unconscious. Thus, the importance of cultural forces in international relations is no less fundamental because they are often concealed and overlaid.

Peace is the realization of the full potentialities of those phases of culture which unite men and give them a sense of human brotherhood. War on the other hand represents the effort to obstruct the channels of this deep-flowing human intercourse, to exploit the lesser differences, rather than the greater unities.

41

CHAPTER VII

EMOTION

EMOTION is the third element consistently present in international relations. Like culture it has not had adequate explicit recognition. It nonetheless plays a vital role.

Anglo-American tradition avoids, so far as possible, the public display of emotion. Consequently there is a strong tendency to treat the subject with silence. Moreover, modern psychological studies have concentrated so heavily upon the abnormal that emotion has been given a false "scientific" handicap. The emotional life, however, is as valid a part of human experience as reason itself.

We perceive truth not only logically but appreciatively. Emotion, therefore, is a normal complement to reason. Neither is a substitute for the other. Only under abnormal and pathological influences are they competitive. Man is not less than reasonable because emotion plays an active part in his life. On the contrary, he is more than reasonable. Emotion should not make him irrational, but perceptive in addition to being rational. Each quality is necessary to redress the balance of the other, and the tensions between them are as requisite and inevitable as the pull of the opposite poles in electricity.

The ancients identified the good, the true, and the beautiful; it was a profound synthesis. When we seek to destroy it, we assault truth. Any comprehensive estimate of life recognizes the emotions as bringing joy, color, and appreciation into the realm of human experience. In normal persons, reason and emotion are each capable of discipline and refinement, and when soundly developed they are mutually enriching, one to the other. Emotion furnishes the impulse and the drive, reason the governing and controlling stability.

In international affairs emotion is one of the elements which may exercise either a positive or a negative influence. Indeed no other exemplifies in such high degree the simultaneous capacity for positive and negative action. Love and hate lie close together in the life circle; an individual or a nation passes from one to the other with astonishing facility. The relations between the United States and Great Britain illustrate the fundamental attachment of sentimental ties and also the inevitable irritations of family intimacies.

Expressed positively, emotion exhibits amazing powers of attachment; employed negatively, it can be just as strong a force in dividing men. Its roots are so deep in human life that its influence when magnified beyond normal limits may overwhelm reason and defy rational control. In the years following the American Revolution, hatred of Britain, from whom we had won independence, and love of France, who had helped us, made the development of a rational policy difficult. That was why Washington, in his Farewell Address, warned that "permanent, inveterate antipathies against particular nations and passionate attachments for others should be excluded." He was appealing to reason as a check upon emotion.

However powerful emotion may be in international relations, it has one critical weakness. As culture is the most stable, emotion is the most volatile of the basic elements. Fear of this quality is the reason statesmen have made a continuous effort to eliminate or at least subordinate this factor. The same characteristic has made it, on the other hand, the natural instrument of the demagogue, who exploits revolutionary periods by emotional appeals. In an age like the present, marked by revolt from reason, when, as Nietzsche urged, feeling takes precedence over reason, propagandists for the dictators have naturally sought to exploit emotion, in the belief that the actions of men "originate from their feelings."

"To lead means: to be able to move masses," wrote Hitler. Goebbels said propaganda has only one purpose, "the conquest of the masses." The masses, in the Nazi mind, are aroused not by reason, but by sentiment. Consequently propaganda in the Axis states has become almost wholly an attempt to play upon emotion. There is a legitimate and proper appeal to the emotions, but if it is to develop a sound public opinion, the appeal must be to the higher emotions. The dictators, on the contrary, have deliberately pandered to the lowest in mankind; it is a reflection of their contempt for the masses. They have sought to inflame the passions rather than to sensitize appreciation; they have fostered spiritual blindness instead of moral insight.

In its original sense, propaganda involved the spread of ideas and was not hostile to reason. Ideas can be propagated as well as feelings can be aroused. Often the two go together. The Declaration of Independence was a reasoned statement, but it was cast in an emotional frame to enhance its power and give it the widest possible appeal. It was a mighty piece of propaganda and a document of profound importance in the history of that art. The founders of our republic had the right balance between feeling and thought. Modern dictators want only feelings as the basis of a commitment; academics sometimes speak as though thought alone were enough. Judgment, however, consists of a synthesis of the two.

The Declaration of Independence illustrates perfectly the method of developing a public opinion at once informed and stirred to action. But dictators want action, without the control of informed opinion. They do not trust people with ideas; that is one reason the intelligentsia were so persistently assaulted; it was essential to destroy the prestige of independent thinkers. Totalitarian leaders want masses committed to ideologies, which are quite different from ideas. "By clever, persistent propaganda," said Hitler, "even heaven can be represented to a people as hell and the most wretched life as paradise." The aim is to develop mobs passionately attached to the symbols of the state, the party, the leader, ready to act with blind obedience and unwavering devotion. That is one of the evidences of the primitivism of this false "new order," for the emotional imbalance is stimulated just when literacy has become all but universal, and when the means for public discussion and the rational development of public opinion have become fully available.

The recent attempt to make propaganda into an exceedingly important instrument in international policy is popularly thought to be a characteristic manifestation of "total" war. It is often spoken of as though it were something new in history. Even on the emotional level, propaganda is an old weapon in the armory of strategy and glitters only because it has been newly burnished. When Gideon "and the hundred men that were with him came into the outside of the camp . . . they blew the trumpets and brake the pitchers that were in their hands." That was a device to convince the defenders there was an overwhelming host moving to the assault; it was an early manifestation of the war of nerves. It was an effort to demoralize the home front by fear; psychological warfare is a new name for an age-old reality.

Two factors have been responsible for the belief that modern propaganda is different not only in amount but also in kind from anything history has seen before. The first is the application of scientific psychology to the process. The various tricks of the trade have been classified and described; the techniques have been refined and elaborated. On the other hand, the processes of propaganda analysis and counter-propaganda have been strengthened in like degree. The historic and inevitable tendency to balance offense with defense is nowhere more clearly evident. The apparent successes of the method of propaganda have been so great and the warnings against it so shrill that the public has become oversensitive, even allergic, to this weapon. Under those circumstances the results are sometimes actually the reverse of the intention.

As part of the defeatist trend which has been so marked in the democracies during recent years, it was believed that totalitarian countries were more effective in propaganda than democracies. Indeed all "foreign" propaganda was thought more subtle and more potent than our own. Dr. Goebbels became almost a figure of legend. It is true that Nazi propaganda was more ruthless, more insistent, and more aggressive than ours. It is true, also, that it was organized upon a scale and employed with an intensity unique in history. But after temporary successes, the reaction became so violent that any statement from Germany was

suspect, and thus emotional resistance was greatly stimulated. In short, the overemployment of the instrument carried its own penalty. Momentary tactical success was ultimately more than offset by strategic failure.

The second factor which encourages the myth of the
"new" propaganda is modern communication. The agencies for its spread have certainly been enormously increased
and its physical suppression made all but impossible. The
radio, in particular, is heard across boundaries and facilitates the work of the propagandist. This process likewise
carries its own corrective. The channels are open in both
directions and counter-propaganda gains new opportuni-
ties. Of course tyrannous governments do more to suppress
receipt of material than liberal governments. But that is a
reflection of the basic faiths and the characteristic methods
of the two types of government rather than of the power
of propaganda.

The new methods of communication have certain weaknesses for propaganda purposes, as well as strengths. Broadcasts are available to a very wide audience—not alone to
the group for whom the propaganda is intended, but to
many more besides. Material designed for home consumption is heard abroad; its falsity is often clear, its weaknesses
are apparent, and responses can be framed. Similarly, matter designed to influence foreign listeners is sometimes
more avidly consumed at home. Under such circumstances
a government may become a slave to public passion—the
prisoner of its own propaganda. Then it is forced to do
things its leaders know to be unwise, even futile. That is
another illustration of a momentary tactical gain which
involves an ultimate strategic loss.

There was a third factor which gave totalitarian propaganda a real advantage. It was due neither to skill nor to the agencies employed, but resulted from the coincidence of the assaults upon the democracies with the defeatist spirit which dominated those countries. Such a spirit did not exist twenty-five years before. The second half of the nineteenth century was an age of democratic triumph. Its successes were so transcendent that its failures were discounted. The mood of exaltation, however, is often—one might say normally—followed by one of depression.

The period of triumph had been long; the succeeding reaction, not so much an economic depression as one of spirit, was violent and protracted. During the era of victory, shortcomings were acknowledged but discounted; during the era of defeatism, weaknesses were exaggerated. When the last war was won, the world was supposed to be safe for democracy. Failure of Armageddon to prove the battle to end all wars, failure of the peace to be perfect and perpetual, failure of "normalcy" to cure all social and economic ills led to disillusionment. The loss of faith in reason accelerated the decline in democratic prestige.

The impact of totalitarian propaganda—Communist, Fascist, and Nazi—fell just at the moment when the leaders of democracy had lost faith in the resiliency of their economy, walked in fear of social upheaval, and tended toward cynicism regarding the rational foundation of the democratic process itself. So the specious orderliness of publicized "plans" among the totalitarians was contrasted with the "chaos" of individualism. The brutality, the ruthlessness, the hardships, and the inefficiencies of those plans in actual operation were not adequately recognized. In short, there was a strong tendency to look chiefly at the credit side of the foreign ledger and at the debit side of the do-

48

mestic. In the face of this prevailing defeatism, the astonishing fact is not that totalitarian propaganda achieved some successes, but that its victories were ultimately so transient.

Much emphasis has been laid upon the power of totalitarian propaganda to create confusion among those who would oppose it, and there is evidence to support that idea. On the other hand, it has not been sufficiently emphasized that some of its power to confuse is a mere reflection of totalitarian confusion. It is inherent, not deliberate. The solidarity of the Nazi state is a myth. There are uncounted thousands of Germans who feel no loyalty to its shibboleths. There are others who accept Nazi rule pending something better. The war between the party and the army is bitter. The church, both Roman Catholic and Evangelical, is deeply at odds with the party. Even party leaders disagree. The Führer himself is inconsistent. This inherent confusion is inevitably reflected in the propaganda which often creates confusion because the source is itself confused. In the long run this will result in strategic failure.

The power of propaganda is not always negative. In fact its negative employment is an abuse. Our Good Neighbor policy has a propaganda phase of great significance. The policy itself is a diplomatic reality; its expression assumes many forms. The expansion of cultural relations, the exchange of art and artists, music and musicians, students and teachers, the distribution of American movies, the use of broadcasts—these and hundreds of other factors have created a better emotional setting for the appeal to reason through diplomacy. From a perfectionist standpoint there is much to be desired; nevertheless these activities have proved successful in competition with Nazi techniques.

STRATEGY OF PEACE

Moreover, it must be remembered that propaganda in its positive rational form—the dissemination of ideas—is not so transitory in its effects as the emotional outpourings of a Goebbels. It may not have the tactical brilliance shown by the propaganda of confusion, but it has a long-run strategic solidity lacking in the negative type. It facilitates successful diplomacy and opens the way for the exploitation of economic measures in a manner which adds greatly to their effectiveness. Its very lack of over-organization, the absence of too much self-consciousness and pressure give its results a depth and balance which the propaganda of confusion cannot attain.

Propaganda has both gained and lost by the application of scientific principles and technological devices. It remains powerful in proportion as it is employed in behalf of a national strategy clearly perceived, ardently pursued, reflecting deep faith. It is more successful if the enemy has any tendency to defeatism, or if rifts in the opponents' solidarity can be exploited. It must be timed to perfection and coordinated with other means or the results, however desirable, evaporate rapidly. When used in a positive way to create understanding and cement friendship, propaganda is more stable than when its purposes are merely negative—the creation of confusion and the stimulation of hate.

CHAPTER VIII

ECONOMIC ACTIVITY

THE fourth of the elements always present in national
and international policy is economic activity. Like the two
preceding factors, economic activity may be used positively
or negatively. In the most general terms, the positive use
looks to the creation of wealth, the negative to the exercise of pressure. Next to the direct employment of force,
economic leverage has come to be regarded as the most
powerful implement of modern political strategy. The
positive phase tends toward peace and the negative employment of economic leverage makes for war. Any gen-
eralization requires qualification, and this is no exception
to that rule; nonetheless it offers a sound working precept.

Every age has its conflicts of ideas, which only time re-
solves. And as in every conflict the victor bears the scars
of battle, so, also, the ideas which become dominant have
been modified by the stress and strain of the tussle. Logic
suffers in the achievement of practical solutions.

In our own time three sets of economic ideas have been
contending for mastery. There is the classical economics
of capitalism which postulates mutual profit through enterprise. There is the revived dogma of mercantilism
which teaches that what is profit for one is loss for another, and that profit is significant primarily as a source
and symbol of power. And there is the Marxian thesis
which rejects profit and demands production for use. All

51

these systems have been developed with logical completeness in exposition, but none ever appears in its pure and unadulterated form in actual experience. Nevertheless they represent foci around which cluster forces inevitably in conflict. When one speaks of economic activity under such circumstances, there is always a question regarding the basic presuppositions, for the consideration of any given problem in the terms of these three frames of reference is as though men were talking in three separate languages, each of which was only imperfectly understood by the others, if understood at all.

We are apt to think that our age is more confused about its basic presuppositions than its predecessors. That impression is due to the gaps in modern knowledge of the past. When issues are settled the struggle by means of which they were resolved is often forgotten, merely because the modern mind bcomes absorbed in other matters of more immediate concern. The moving panorama of human activity is so vast and so swift that history can be understood only by being simplified. Every act and every thought and every person who ever lived are part of the fabric of mankind's experience. But the effort to encompass so tremendous a range defeats itself and we fall back, therefore, upon simplifications which allow us to deal with the problem, but which inevitably distort it.

We look back and speak of the feudal system, for example, as though the term had a definite content, whereas it was so various in its manifestations as almost to defy definition. It is customary to assume that within the area in which it existed its institutions were substantially uniform, but in different places they were marked by more contrasts than similarities. It is assumed, too, that the period to which it applied had a high degree of uniformity. On the contrary it embraced centuries of constant change. Like every living thing, feudalism was dying as it grew, waning as it increased. We can approach an understanding of it only by neglecting differences; as we progress in knowledge the differences become more essential to full comprehension, and their disregard requires correction.

Thus the understanding of the past always requires reservations as to the precise meaning of terms. Without initial precision of meaning, we cannot discuss them. But if that precision is carried too far, it misrepresents instead of enlightens. When this common experience is applied to our present circumstances, it is evident that confusion regarding economic presuppositions was characteristic of times past. It is nothing peculiar to our age. We should view the clash of ideas and the rivalry of systems as an inevitable mark of human intercourse.

Under the dominant presuppositions of the last century and a half, the central function of economic activity—its normal result—has been the creation of wealth; not alone the wealth of profits, nor of stocks, bonds, and "securities," but the real wealth of goods, durable and consumable, which enrich the standard of life of workingman as well as capitalist. If it were possible to consider economic activity in those terms exclusively, it would be evident that it has no inherent political objective whatever.

Even in its purest form, however, the creation of wealth has significant political implications, conscious or otherwise. As a kind of by-product national prestige is enhanced by wealth, which in that way lends support to diplomacy. Moreover it enables a nation to afford resort to force and to support its allies when that becomes necessary. Great wealth is based upon extensive resources, large productive power, a high degree of economic organization, and all those factors are of importance in the "war potential" of a nation.

The positive employment of economic energy makes for peace largely because the production of wealth is based upon a division of labor which transcends international boundaries. If uneconomic political obstacles are not erected, goods flow freely across political lines as, for example, among the states of our union. Internationally, this results in an "open door" policy, growing wealth for all participants, and an interdependence among them that supplies a mutual interest in peaceful activity. Under those circumstances the sharp distinction between the "have" and the "have not" nations tends to decline, and may become of relatively little practical importance. There is no reason, moreover, that ideological differences and contrasting political forms need become barriers to trade. The long history of American trade with the petty despotisms of the Far East illustrates the point. The British free trade policy of the nineteenth century made possible a worldwide commerce with many countries having a vast variety of governments.

The classical "liberal" position fitted that pattern of experience. Its devotees hoped for a beneficial political result in international relations. Richard Cobden expounded the idea in these words: "Nations must be brought into mutual dependence by the supply of each other's wants. There is no other way of counteracting the antagonism of language and race. It is God's own method of producing an entente cordiale, and no other plan is worth a farthing." It will be observed that he considered the power of attraction of mutual benefit superior in effectiveness to very strong forces of separatism. The economic bond seemed to him a kind of divine antidote to the confusions of Babel. It is clear, in retrospect, that this expectation was too optimistic; it was founded upon an overestimate of the positive influence of economic activity. The error was, so to speak, the equal and opposite of the more recent expectation that economic leverage could control aggressors and maintain peace by economic penalties. Both points of view gave too much authority to this element.

Concentration on the positive aspect of economic activity—increasing wealth—permits great international investments without the political consequences of economic "penetration." Despite recent assumptions to the contrary, international investment is not synonymous with economic imperialism. For example, there was no political motive of any consequence in the heavy British investment in several American railroads. Those investments were made before the United States was regarded as a world power, and before the "diplomatic revolution" as a result of which Britain and the United States cooperated actively in international affairs. Yet there was no exploitation involved; capital was in search of profit, and the fact that a "rival" nation was developed as an incident to that transaction did not deter investment. Both countries, in fact, benefited, and there can be no question whatever that the exchange strengthened their common interests and helped offset their natural differences. It was, in short, an aid to peace between them, though by no means the decisive factor. Its political consequences were incidental and mostly beneficent.

It is obvious on the other hand that investments which

in appearance are almost indistinguishable may originate from, or subsequently acquire, quite different motives and, consequently, produce sinister political results. Whereas loans on a positive basis are economic in their results, loans on a negative basis may constitute an attack upon the political integrity of a weaker power. The positive and beneficial employment of international loans has been made more and more difficult by some very bitter experiences, suspicion as to motives in particular instances, and the progressively defensive attitude toward capitalism. Fear of being accused of imperialism has led strong powers, particularly the United States, to lend only feeble diplomatic support to investments abroad. Weaker nations have sometimes taken advantage of this diffidence and appropriated valuable properties with inadequate compensation. Such acts constitute exploitation in reverse; the strong are abused by the weak. The effective employment of international investment on a positive basis is correspondingly discouraged.

Sometimes the positive employment of economic energy carries direct and purposeful constructive political implications. Loans for currency stabilization of a foreign power offer a case in point; they have frequently contributed to the wealth of both nations and to the stability of their political relationships. The nineteenth century, and to a great degree even the twentieth, saw many international transactions which stimulated the productivity of one country and the trade of another. Complementary economies make for mutual advantage, and therefore for peace.

The beneficial effects of the positive employment of economic forces are so transparent and so simple that the inevitable question arises, "Why is economic energy so rarely used positively in international strategy?" The difficulty is partly intellectual. Perhaps the central mental snag is the failure really to believe that both parties can gain by a single transaction. Despite logical demonstrations to the contrary, a feeling survives that profit must be the result of exploitation. Mercantilism, the dominant economic system of the eighteenth century, was founded upon the dogma that mutual profit was a contradiction in terms.

There must be something deeply persuasive in that feeling, for it has never been wholly eradicated. The nineteenth century saw it logically destroyed and virtually abandoned as a policy—but only briefly. In the twentieth century the dogma reappeared in forms scarcely less crude than those which were thought to have been outgrown. Indeed the period since the last war has with some justification been called a neo-mercantilist age. The heavy emphasis upon "favorable" balances of trade, the cornering of gold by a few countries, high "protective" tariffs, exchange controls, quotas, and restrictions of many kinds all illustrate the same tendency to return to mercantilist practices, even when its system of ideas was not explicitly avowed.

The vicious aspect of this tenacious theory is that it inculcates the idea that in every exchange one party must get the better of the other, his gain being the other's loss. In this system it is thought that trade does not increase wealth, but merely transfers it. Therefore the acquisition of wealth becomes identified with enlarging power on one side and increasing weakness on the other. Trade ceases to be mutually beneficial and so a reinforcement of peace; it becomes an instrument of victory for one, defeat for the other—a warlike idea.

There must be some reason for the persistence of a theory which is economically and morally pernicious. Perhaps the explanation lies in the fact that though liberalism proved the mercantilist dogma logically untenable, classical economists overlooked an important reality. Psychologically mercantilism reflects the importance of other factors besides profit which doctrinaire liberalism neglected. Motives are never pure; they are always mixed. So economic activity is never employed exclusively for the creation of wealth, however defined. For beyond a limited accumulation, wealth alone soon ceases to be a valid objective. Man's power to consume with enjoyment is far from infinite. Extravagance in the consumption of wealth cloys and brings its own defeat. The world has been continuously reminded by religion, by observation, and by literature that "you can't take it with you."

There are in fact many potent motives in addition to economic profit. Prestige, power, and numerous intrinsically irrelevant, though humanly desirable, factors enter as additions to or substitutes for the search for wealth as such. Accepting economic gain as the sole goal, as did the classical economists, was as fallacious from a psychological point of view as was the one-sided profit of mercantilism from the intellectual standpoint.

The central weakness of the classical theory of economics, therefore, was its overemphasis upon wealth as the controlling motive. Strangely enough, it shared this fallacy with its arch enemy, Marxian socialism, which was based upon economic determinism. It would have horrified Cobden to be bracketed with Marx; the contrasts are many, but an undue accent upon economic motivation was common to both, though Marx was more extreme in this, as in other

58

respects. Doubtless the error arose in both instances from the overwhelming impact of the industrial revolution. Just as the revolutions in transportation and communication have often thrown our contemporaries off their mental balance, so the increase in the wealth of the world was so great and so rapid that monetary gain was thrown out of perspective. New phenomena, or those which appear to be new, are always overestimated by contemporaries. It is not surprising that so marked a development as the industrial revolution should have overinfluenced both schools of economic thought, however much they differed in other respects.

Wealth, although desirable, fulfills only one of man's wants, and by no means the greatest. The "scorched earth" policy pursued by China, the deliberate and systematic sacrifice of wealth in the interests of independence, is one very dramatic illustration of a fundamental fact. The yearning for freedom, zeal for religious liberty, a sense of loyalty to the homeland—many motives which have no tincture of profit about them—are profoundly influential. The "economic man" was a myth just as was the "proletarian man" or "class."

A generation which has heard "security" and "safety first" dinned into its ears, as though those were the ultimate ideals of mankind, is now summoned to fight. Thus in changed circumstances the inadequacy of ideas long dominant becomes all too apparent; no war was ever won by an army or navy under a banner emblazoned "Safety First"! So, also, the hope that mutual interest in the creation of wealth would overcome all opposing forces and pave the pathway to peace has been proved to have had wholly inadequate foundations. Nonetheless, the mutual production of wealth, used in conjunction with other methods, is an effective implement of strategy.

The logical deficiencies of mercantilism and the psychological shortcomings of classical economics help explain the mixture of positive and negative factors in economic tactics. It is easy to demonstrate that the mixture is incoherent and self-defeating, but it has so far proved impossible to persuade any nation to complete coherence.

Sometimes, contrary to all reason, it is insisted that war creates wealth, or at least that it pays economic dividends. The notion of a positive result from negative activity defies logic but not yearning. An inscription on Pitt's Guildhall monument which declares that he united commerce with war and made the former flourish embodies such a notion. Common discussion today speaks of the Japanese aggression against the Netherlands Indies as the seizure of their vast wealth. Similarly, as the Germans advanced into the Soviet Union there was a constant stream of statistics to show the "profit" on the transaction. Every bushel of grain and every ton of ore in the captured territory was set down as an asset for the next thousand years; the gains, it was implied, would soon outweigh the costs.

This doctrine was, of course, the root idea of imperialism. The theory was that the extravagance involved in conquest was temporary, whereas the profits of exploitation would be permanent. If that doctrine were sound, the costs might not be out of proportion to the benefits. Temporary extravagance might ultimately be compensated by long-range gains.

The error in the reasoning lay in the assumption of permanence. Winds have blown the pollen of nationalism too far, and fertilized the seeds of revolt. The American

Revolution was resistance to exploitation; the same phenomenon has been repeated so often and in so many forms that the economic fallacy of imperialism is usually admitted. If revolt, active or passive, does not put an end to exploitation, the effort of rival powers to break into the closed system and reap the fruits of others' labors has the same effect. If one nation treats a region as booty, another is certain to look at it in the same light and seek to acquire it. The long record of colonial wars fully illustrates that statement of the world's experience. The net effect is the reverse of imperialistic expectation; extravagance is permanent and profits are temporary.

A characteristic of the last quarter century was that it regarded economic power too exclusively in negative terms. Economic "sanctions," for example, were expected to give the League of Nations effective control of aggressors. Thus far, historically speaking, economic pressure has not fulfilled the hopes of its proponents. At its best it has been a subsidiary instrument of strategy. Perhaps its fundamental weakness arises from the fact that economic warfare is, in the truest sense of the phrase, a contradiction in terms. It involves the deliberate misuse of the functions of production and distribution. It causes dislocations which, especially if long continued and ardently applied, create a new situation at home as well as in the enemy nations. The consequence is the substitution of one set of unhealthy and disturbing conditions for another; sometimes the new are even more distracting than the old. In this sense it is an expedient which rarely achieves, indeed it often actually defeats, the attainment of its strategic objective.

CHAPTER IX

FORCE

THE last of the five elements is force. Force is indispensable in all political organizations, and therefore bound to enter into international relations. In ideal circumstances force appears only as a symbol—as the mace is displayed in the British Parliament, and as the beautifully uniformed Swedish policeman patrols an orderly community—a reminder that force, present only in ceremonial form, exists in ready reserve.

Internationally, there is a "war potential" for every nation. The size of its population, the character of its resources, the nature of its economic organization, and all the factors capable of mobilization exert force. In times of tension there is emphasis upon preparedness, and we speak of force in being; when the tension snaps and fighting breaks out, we have force in action.

Force is actually most successful in advancing the policy of a nation when there is no need to use it actively. Wisely employed as a reserve support of political action, force is not directly destructive, though always costly. Once made a major instrument and employed actively, it tends to become an end in itself. It is so dramatic, its effects are so apparent that one can easily succumb to the phrase heard so often today: "Nothing counts but force." If that mood takes possession, force is certain to over-reach its strategic objective; many a nation has burnt a house to roast a pig.

The means become more important than the end. When that happens, a new problem is created which is more difficult to solve than the old.

If force is used actively, the disastrous effects upon economic power are almost infinite. Confusion in wealth-producing enterprises is artificially created; energy is diverted to the armed services and war industries. Millions of men are taken from their customary employment, their work habits disorganized and skills blunted, their capacity for normal adjustment dislocated, and their whole rhythm of life altered. In the second place, many industries must be retooled to make munitions rather than articles of peace, a retooling process which takes a long time even under the urgent pressures of war, with government subsidies and negligent treatment of costs. But the retooling procedure, when reversed, will not face the same urgent requirements for speed and will have to be done as efficiently and economically as possible lest it lead to bankruptcy. In the third place, the closing of the normal lanes of trade leads to the increased employment of known synthetics and substitutes and the enormous development of new products and processes. Consequently the post-war world faces a dilemma: shall it return to the original sources of supply and let all the new production machinery for substitutes go to waste, or shall it continue to manufacture synthetic rubber, for example, and the thousands of other *ersatz* materials? Either program may prove costly and wasteful. In the fourth place, the land and its resources may be seriously impaired for as much as twenty-five years after a "scorched earth" policy has been applied. In the fifth place, enormous productive capacities are utterly destroyed, impoverishing the whole world in a shocking degree. The use of force, that is to say, increases tremendously the disaster of economic warfare.

Nothing better illustrates the contemporary discount upon historical perspective than the current ideas regarding force. One would suppose that only recently had it somehow got out of hand; that it used to be a fairly precise instrument of policy; that wars could be planned for, political objectives carried through to predetermined ends, and then force could be liquidated. It is assumed that now somehow force has suddenly acquired instrumentalities so terrible that its results are more disastrous than ever before. The power of destruction of giant guns and monster bombs is great, but the present view overlooks the fact that constructive power has kept pace. Once a sacked city was a perpetual ruin. One has only to visit the historical monuments of the past to see the marks of force upon them. Today the work of reconstruction is begun before destruction has ceased. The idea has become general that the blitz is entirely new and that the speed of force has been tremendously accelerated. We forget that Alexander conquered the world before he was thirty and that Napoleon, in a very brief span of years, mastered Europe, invaded Africa, and was looking toward America. The truth is that force, when used as an instrument of policy, has always produced situations so new that the original objectives are lost.

It is one of the tragedies of human life that in the midst of battle, when men think they understand the issues for which they are fighting, the real issues are quite different. An interesting book by Dr. Richard C. Cabot was entitled *What Men Live By*. Someone should press further the observation of Antoine de Saint Exupéry in *Wind, Sand and Stars* on what men die for. All too often men have laid down their lives for false issues, because the heat of battle generates its own issues and so confuses perspective that when the war is over, even a victorious war, the peace seldom conforms to the original objectives. It deals instead with new problems which have arisen out of the conflict itself. The longer the war is carried on, the more perspective is obscured. Victory tends to become an end in itself rather than an opportunity so to organize our lives as to avoid fighting again. It is significant that we celebrate Armistice Day as a holiday, but no one pays the slightest attention to the day when peace was proclaimed. Perhaps that is why the "peace" proved to be only an armistice.

After the last World War there was a stream of books of which Ernest Hemingway's *Farewell to Arms*, Remarque's *All Quiet on the Western Front*, Zweig's *The Case of Sergeant Grischa*, and Anderson and Stalling's *What Price Glory* are typical. These books were denunciations, underlining the point that desperate as were the encounters, bloody and terrifying as was the fighting, so far as achieving the original objectives was concerned, it was a sham—not a sham in the movie sense, wherein men mowed down by machine guns leap up at the call of the director to be mowed down again in a better light, but sham in the sense that the war actually proved to be about other things than those which precipitated it. Although those authors had too contemporary a view, the indubitable fact of which they complained was part of the inescapable stuff of history, did they but know it.

The employment of force, furthermore, brings an inevitable irrationality into conclusions; it appears so overwhelming in its immediate effects that the permanent power of reason is eclipsed. Moreover, when it approaches its most violent phase, the use of force tends to a reversal of the moral order and a proclamation that might makes right. If, for example, the successes of the Soviet Union were to continue without any pause, and if, contrary to expectation, the Red Army were actually to whip Germany without equal Allied gains on other European fronts, it would give the Soviet Union an influence upon the structure of the post-war world out of scale to its experience, its wisdom, its real interests, and other factors which normally—that is to say, when there is dependence upon the economical use of the five basic elements—would have great weight.

With reason, force alone among these elements shares the quality of having only one direction. Its direction, however, is opposite to that of reason, for reason is always a positive element. The fruits of force are always negative. Force can destroy Hitler, but it gives no hint regarding what should be done next. Its logic, therefore, can never be constructive. Its employment is necessary to make peace possible, but paradoxically contributes nothing positive to that end, and becomes, in that sense at least, an enemy to integrated national and international strategy.

Above all it is important to remember that force cannot be permanently decisive. Military action, for example, may win living space. But the application of force may leave a sullen and resentful conquered minority, the control of which requires the relentless application of additional force; the situation becomes more and more irritated, less and less subject to rational solution. The Irish problem, for example, is the harvest of long-continued use of force. It is a reminder of the wisdom of Talleyrand in his report to the Directory in 1798 when he said: "Force of arms is transitory, whereas hatred lives on."

66

There are those who, failing to learn this lesson, would have us permanently occupy the defeated nations and continue indefinitely to hold them under strict surveillance. They rest their faith on force and neglect the real outcome of any such program. Disagreement with that proposal is not the result of sympathy for those who launched so much horror upon the world. The real danger lies in the state of mind which must be developed here at home if the suggested procedure is to be tolerated and supported. A police mentality would be necessary to operate an international gestapo. We would need to inculcate habits of thought and action which are the antithesis of those appropriate either to freedom or to democracy.

Certainly force is at best a crude instrument with which to fashion and refashion civilization. It is so violent and so unwieldy that it alters the very fabric of life. Such knowledge should make it plain that hopes for peace following the prolonged use of force must be adapted to the resulting limitations and imperfections. We cannot expect to escape from hell into utopia in one stride. Striving for peace is not an episode; it must be a perpetual quest.

In summary it seems clear that war and peace are merely phases in the pursuit of national and international policy. The distinctions between them, sharp enough at the extremes, are almost indistinguishable at the mean; war breeds even while peace seems flourishing, and peace is incubated even during the fury of war. The secret of statesmanship in peace is to identify and neutralize the tendencies toward negativism, such as the substitution of will for reason, selfish nationalism for a broader outlook, hate for tolerance, embargoes for the "open door," and violence for the symbols of force. The secret of statesmanship in war is to exploit the use of force for the advancement of the ends suggested by reason, for the spread of universal culture, and for the employment of economic power to enrich the whole world.

It requires the cooperation of all nations to maintain the peace, but the misbehavior of one, unless checked by all, can result in war. Peace, therefore, is secure only so long as states are willing to risk war to preserve it. It was the tragedy of the last twenty years that this was precisely what they were unwilling to do. Those who cherished peace held to its form long after the substance was gone; they clung to the empty shell from which the richness had departed. Only the future can reveal whether the world has learned the lesson.

PART II
AMERICAN COMMITMENTS

Chapter X

PERSPECTIVE

A fair survey of American foreign policy demands a sense of perspective. Policies must be viewed in the light of today's crisis, but not in those terms alone. Sound judgments require that they be considered as dynamic forces, taking their shape from the past, in continuous process of reformation, and destined to be projected into the future. As Secretary Hull said in his April 9, 1944, exposition of American foreign policy: "It has continuity of basic objectives because it is rooted in the traditions and aspirations of our people. It must, of course, be applied in the light of experience and the lessons of the past." So vast and complex are the problems that policies will never be entirely clear and consistent. They can never be perfectly adapted to their present aims, for sometimes events outrun our minds, while at other times our imaginations outstrip reality.

A number of factors make just judgments regarding American international relations particularly difficult at this time. Three deflecting influences may be mentioned as having a marked effect upon current appraisals. The first is the mood of pessimism in which the United States was long plunged, the second is the vogue of geopolitics, and the third is the war itself.

The general temper of the time always affects contemporary opinion on particular subjects. It is especially important when, as occasionally happens in history, men get the idea that they are living in a "new" age. Experience is discounted by the feeling that present events are unique, that they are introducing a new phase in the life of the world for which history supplies no valid precedents to guide thought. This has been such an age in a peculiar degree. In politics, the Soviet Union has furnished a "new" kind of state, Hitler proclaimed a "new" order. Even those who reject the thesis that either of these innovations rides the "wave of the future" nonetheless repudiate the status quo, refuse to tolerate "outmoded" ideas, and look for some new political, economic, and social synthesis.

Nothing better illustrates human capacity to move simultaneously in opposite directions than the doubts and pessimism which have marked the recent period of great scientific and technological accomplishment. The syntheses of pure science have supplied some of the most brilliant achievements of the human mind. In applied science and medicine accomplishments have been so extraordinary that they appear almost as miracles. Technological advance has been more swift than ever before in history, and public awareness and anticipation even swifter. Such an outburst of energy might well have led to expressions of optimism and confidence. A social, economic, and political organization capable of initiating and supporting such amazing developments might be expected to be regarded as remarkable also. In politics, however, the initiative was surrendered to the Communists and the Fascists; their fiery energy and insistent assertiveness overshadowed the more substantial long-run advances of democracy, and led to doubts regarding its effectiveness. American political institutions, whose emergence had dominated the nineteenth century, were heavily discounted in the third and fourth decades of the twentieth.

The shadow was made deeper by the gloom of a severe economic recession, which not only mastered business, but even worse, dominated thought. This depression was asserted to be not only longer in duration and more severe in degree, but different in kind from any that had preceded it. The contrast between the marvels of invention and production, upon the one hand, and unemployment, upon the other, deepened pessimism. It made men fear that capacity to produce had outrun ability to distribute and consume. This doubled the doubts and magnified the fears. When the aggressive nations insisted they had mastered unemployment, there was too little analysis of their methods and the collateral results; thus the prestige of democracies was lowered still more. To many minds the "new" governments indeed rode the "wave of the future"; the revolution of our time presaged the twilight of democracy.

Often judgments regarding our diplomacy between the two wars are colored by the fact that they follow this long period of national retreat. The optimism and buoyancy characteristic of the American temper in earlier times have been conspicuously absent in recent appraisals of foreign policy. Confidence in the future has been shaky. Imperialism, economic or political, the concept of "manifest destiny," whatever the crudities or brashness of those ideas, at least reflected courage, faith, and confidence. It would never have occurred to Daniel Webster to evaluate American policy in terms of a balance sheet. He had too keen an awareness of the dynamic quality of the American ideal to attempt to express it through so inapt a medium.

The prevalent mood of the last few years seriously warps

perspective; pessimism is a crooked mirror. The tendency now to view our world position in the static and coldly calculating terms of a balance sheet is the natural product of doubt and waning confidence. Only under such circumstances would men turn to a medium that takes no account of growth and potentialities, but concerns itself exclusively with static elements. Only in a dark mood do we assess policy in material terms, leaving out of account the intangible elements of reason, culture, and moral commitment.

There are always important assets no bookkeeping system adequately reveals. For example, many great corporations show an item, "Patents—$1.00." It is a formal recognition that patents are assets, but if they were really worth only one dollar, the business would go to smash. They are so dynamic in character that their value cannot be expressed by a fiscal device. Good will is another live asset; it may be of greatest importance, but it does not appear on a balance sheet. Skill, the most dynamic asset of all, is likewise missing from the ledger. No one would judge a business by the figures alone; he must know many other things about its past, its management, its prospects. It must be assessed as a going concern.

In like manner the balance sheet technique of estimating national policy omits many of its most essential factors. It is fair to say that such a method of appraisal is almost certain to result in the conclusion that our program is insolvent, for the process of evaluation itself reflects doubts regarding our economic and political future; it completely omits spiritual resources, leaves ideals aside as irrelevant, and hesitates to proclaim a resounding and sincere faith in democracy.

The second factor that makes it difficult fairly to survey American foreign policy is the current fashion of geopolitics which looks at historic policy through a crooked lens. Like so many novelties, it assumes a false importance. Some years ago a little book, entitled *Fashion Is Spinach*, developed the sound principle that good design survives fleeting fads. We need to apply that lesson to fashionable ideas; then historical and cultural perspective would save us from surrendering judgment to ephemeral trends in thought. Such ideological fashions have a brief moment in which to exploit their bizarre notions, then the vogue passes swiftly. Technocracy was one such; it consisted in the misuse of important concepts.

Now we have another illustration. Geopolitics is, in fact, a whole cluster of fads, grouped under a single name. The war invites attention to strategic problems, and lends military thinkers an influence which sometimes exceeds their political grasp. Military strategy is heavily dependent upon topographical factors; by a false analogy political strategy is assumed to be equally influenced by geography. On the contrary political action is far less under the control of terrain. For instance, much of the boundary between the United States and Canada is strategically absurd, although politically satisfactory. Military considerations set force over against reason and give little weight to emotion, culture, or even economic activity; but national policy cannot neglect four of its essential elements, concentrating all attention on the fifth.

Geopolitics has developed a technical jargon which gives it a false authority. Its terms, however, are often more impressive than its substance, and it is by no means as scientific as it pretends to be. Behind a solid structure of political geography, to which it calls deserved attention, is concealed a dangerous political philosophy—power politics. These two elements in geopolitics have no necessary relationship to each other; nevertheless it is their union which has appropriated the name and makes geopolitics something different from geography. Moreover, the geographical science and the political philosophy are not mixed in equal proportions; geopolitics contains much more political assumption than geographical substance.

The essence of power politics is very simple; it is that every nation exists by power and its policy should be dedicated to increasing its power. It assumes as proven fact that the "reality" of politics is power. Thus one of the five elements in international relations—force—is exalted above the other four. Reason, culture, emotion, and economic activity are discounted; force, potential or actual, is made the central fact of international life. If that basic premise is correct, if power politics is the true key to sound international relations, not only is American foreign policy bankrupt, but all American history has been based upon error.

Geopolitics seeks to explain how force exploits topography. In its concentration upon physical factors—terrain and force—it not only overlooks or seriously discounts the intangibles, such as reason, culture, and ethics; it also underestimates historical development. It disregards the momentum which the past bequeathed the present. Often, in political life, the intangible and even the unreal are of great importance.

The history of law, for example, cannot be approached successfully without an appreciation of the useful role of fictions in its development. Legal fictions are admitted absurdities which may not be challenged in court. Murder upon the high seas should not go unpunished, but there being no court for the ocean, by a fiction it was asserted

76

that the murder was committed "upon the high seas, to wit in Eastcheap." The obvious untruth could not be questioned because it performed a useful service in giving jurisdiction to a court. Illustrations can be multiplied indefinitely.

In international relations, fictions have proved equally significant. The concept of Western Hemispheric solidarity may be geographically incredible as devotees of geopolitics aver. It is quite true that the United States is farther away from parts of South America than either is from Europe; it is not to be denied that possession of African bases or Atlantic islands by an enemy might cut the lines of United States naval influence. Hemispheric solidarity may be, in a very real sense, a geographic fiction. But within the limitations of human imperfection, it has had a significant political reality for well over a hundred years. It has profoundly and constructively influenced the history of the modern world.

To write off the fundamental experience of Pan Americanism as essentially meaningless merely because it does not correspond with geopolitical dogmas is absurd. Ideas are often more stubborn than physical qualities, and more resistant to change. The human spirit is more potent than any pseudo-scientific determinism, such as geopolitics, can admit. In denying historical realities and insisting that only the tangibles are real, geopolitics gives us another illustration of the modern retreat from reason. Any form of determinism is clearly anti-rational, and therefore anti-democratic; it inevitably is hostile to the spread, and even the existence, of freedom.

The third and most profoundly disturbing element which affects appraisals of policy is the existence of war. Thinking is distorted because war, the culmination of negative elements in life, is the final manifestation of stress and confusion. In the midst of so dramatic a struggle it is all but impossible to make unbiased observations, and it is even harder to arrive at fair evaluations. The present is dimly perceived through the smoke of battle. It is drawn out of focus by the dislocations of economic and political life. Under such conditions men tend to make large generalizations upon short-run experiences, neglecting relevant permanent factors. Some recent writers about American policy have yielded to the temptation to overdramatize the current tragedy. They have reached conclusions at variance with calmer judgments; such wartime opinions will inevitably be radically revised when perspective is restored.

Viewing our policy through lenses warped by these three distortions—pessimism, geopolitics, and war—many Americans are appalled at the range and scale of our commitments in international relations. The most articulate commentator has declared that "in our foreign relations for nearly half a century the United States has been insolvent" because policies and power have not been in balance. In this instance the assertion is so sweeping that it contains its own refutation. During that half century this country gained unqualified recognition as a leading nation of the world. In that period our influence in international trade, finance, and politics grew enormously. The weight of this country in the world balance was decisive in the last war, and bids fair to be equally so in this one. As strength increased, self-restraint kept pace. The Good Neighbor policy replaced the Big Stick; imperialism gave way to reduced commitments; many obligations were contracted rather than expanded; the power to dominate was used less and less. To describe that record by the word "insolvency" drains the term of any significant meaning.

Some observers fear that the maintenance of our international policies will require the militarization of national life. Our world political obligations have sometimes been stated in such terms as to require not a two-ocean navy but a seven-ocean navy. They have been so estimated as to demand not a readiness to arm the civilian population in times of crisis but the perpetuation of a huge standing army. They have been so described as to necessitate not an occasional shift of industrial emphasis from civilian production to munitions and matériel of war but a fundamental reorientation of our economy over a long future.

Presented in cold analytical terms, our international obligations may be made to appear overwhelming. It is pointed out that we have heavy obligations for the total defense of this entire hemisphere, including not only continental United States, Canada, Mexico, Central and South America, but also Greenland and the outlying islands of the Atlantic and Pacific.

Our most sweeping commitment is in the Southern Hemisphere which, it has been argued, is not justified strategically, or on grounds of economic interest, historical affinity, or cultural relationships. It is true that much of South America is not only culturally alien, but economically competitive rather than complementary, and geographically more remote than Europe. Viewed analytically, therefore, under the dogmas of geopolitics this responsibility can be made to appear unreasonable and even irrational. It has been cited as evidence that "the tendency to over-estimate our military strength is a recurring feature in our national psychology, but we have seldom indulged more gloriously

79

than in the famous presidential proclamation" of James Monroe.

We also have long-standing commitments in the Pacific and the Far East, and our deep involvements in the South Pacific and the Antipodes have recently become obvious. We have significant interests in Africa and the Near East and Europe, as the scope of our invasion forces demonstrates. Geographically, economically, and culturally the Far Eastern policy is pictured as irrational. Distances are enormous, the military problems difficult, our economic stake relatively slight, and the cultural relationships negative. Yet, it is pointed out, there has been no isolationism vis-à-vis the Far East, whereas we have been hesitant about making clear advance commitments regarding Europe where our economic interest is paramount, political and cultural relationships are close, and our military power has been tested and proved.

To observers convinced that we have overstepped our power, it appears we have taken the whole world for our province. They imply, moreover, that we have undertaken this enterprise single-handed. These commitments, in short, can be and have been presented in such terms as to make them look like quixotic knight-errantry. When a statement of our foreign policy results in the conclusion that public opinion has been consistently wrong and we and our predecessors have been fools, it is fair to ask whether the description of the facts is accurate and adequate. Such an interpretation suggests our international commitments are being drawn so completely out of perspective that it is not only impossible to support them, but more important, it is impossible even to understand them.

We can help to restore our balance by looking at the

matter from a human point of view. An analogy based upon the realization that national commitments do not differ essentially from personal commitments will assist. If at a given moment in the life of an individual a cross-section survey were made of all his personal obligations—social, economic, political, physical, and moral—that analysis might coincide with severe illness and other adverse environmental factors, such as a business depression. Under those circumstances even the wisest man might be made to look as though he had undertaken too much. A reappraisal a few months later, when his energies were restored, would lead to a different conclusion. A person who never undertook to do more than he could accomplish under the worst imaginable conditions would be the real fool. The overcaution that led the timid soul of the parable to bury his talent in a napkin was not wisdom but folly. To judge a man's commitments only under the most adverse circumstances hides his strength and accents his weakness. That is precisely what many recent appraisers of national policy have done.

The personal analogy, moreover, shows that obligations are neither constant nor uniform. It is the fashion to describe national policies as though all required the support of force. It is an error characteristic of our time to give too little credit to moral leverage or to the power of reason. "A decent respect to the opinions of mankind" is too heavily discounted. These intangibles are written off as "words," whereas the only actualities are those "real enough to be kicked." On such a basis every commitment appears equally vital and binding. But that is not a fair definition of reality; nor does it reflect the true nature of life. Obligations vary enormously in their finality. A few are absolute and involve life itself; some necessitate financial support; others moral influence; still others are transient and require little energy. While commitments tend to accumulate, they do not grow indefinitely. Again the personal analogy makes the point clear. One begins to accept obligations as a child; they pyramid as youth merges into maturity. In proportion as a man plays his full part in the world, those burdens become more onerous, but his capacity grows commensurately. He acquires, first of all, the strength to make them and, second, the judgment to know when to reduce or slough off some of them. Any fair picture of our national policies must take account of the obligations which have been curtailed as well as those which have been expanded.

As a nation we have not simply undertaken larger and larger international responsibilities. Relative to our position in the world today, for example, our commitment regarding Pan America is not so great as it was in 1823. Indeed no modern President has expressed the policy as sharply as Jefferson, who predicted that at no distant day we would "formally require a meridian of partition through the ocean which separates the two hemispheres, on the hither side of which no European gun" could be fired effectively. Not only are we more powerful; the other nations of this hemisphere are also, and we have drawn them into partnership in maintaining the principle that the New World is to be free from colonization and imperialism. We have never fought a war to support our traditional attitude, yet few national policies have survived as long or achieved such signal success.

In order to maintain the thesis that our Pan American policy is "bankrupt" and "illogical" it has been necessary to assert that the British fleet supplied the support which was responsible for its apparent success. That argument is not sound either historically or logically, but it points to a vital consideration. Such a broad policy as ours never stands by itself; it is part of a vast dynamic complex of constantly moving elements. It is dependent not alone upon its own rational validity, upon cultural affinity, or its appeal to mutual economic advantage, much less upon our nation's unilateral possession or use of force. Its capacity to succeed is influenced by the parallel or competing interests of many countries, by their rivalries and preoccupation with other concerns. Though we announced the Monroe Doctrine alone, and had no understanding, even tacit, with any foreign nation, the United States rightfully counted upon those factors. There was ample justification for the assumption that from time to time different interests—but not always those of any single country—would to some extent coincide with our own. That is what happened.

It is an oversimplification so gross as to result in untruth to say that it was always British interest, supported by the British fleet, which "protected" the Monroe Doctrine. That makes it look as though a situation which existed at some given time always existed—a fatal historical error. Through much of the period from 1823 to 1898, seventy-five years, Great Britain was regarded as a potential aggressor against the policy of the United States. During our Civil War, when diplomatic relations with Britain were strained almost to the breaking point, that nation joined in the forceful occupation of Mexican customs-houses, preceding the Maximilian episode. The Venezuela boundary dispute in the administration of Cleveland brought the sharpest threat of the use of force in the whole history of the doctrine.

The historical fact is that a succession of nations—Spain, Britain, France, Germany—challenged the doctrine. Each of them, however, had less to gain by persistently attacking its precepts than we by its elastic but dogged defense with such diplomatic or other support as was available from time to time. It is neither sheer accident nor just plain luck, therefore, that it has never been necessary to fight a war to maintain the Monroe Doctrine. Furthermore our statesmen had good reason to know that if such a war occurred, a European or Asiatic aggressor would find himself fighting not the United States alone, or just American nations; they knew that other enemies of the aggressor would take advantage of his military involvement in this hemisphere to settle old scores elsewhere.

Commitments, that is to say, are neither isolated nor wholly unilateral, although they may appear to be so. That is why it is impossible to make a current balance sheet that has more than transitory validity. Even to possess accuracy for so brief an instant, it must take account not alone of American policy and power, but of the whole pattern of international relations of which it is an integral part. That is why if the wrong moment is chosen for such an evaluation, incorrect conclusions regarding long-term policies will follow. International policies fit into a pattern at once so complex and so compact that any specific one is hard to appraise by itself.

Not only did we shrewdly count upon outside support when essential; we also took care, as time went on, to curtail some of our ambitions. Our forefathers confidently expected that we would annex Cuba; we not only declined to acquire it when it was in our grasp, but we have no intention of ever doing so. Our forebears likewise anticipated the annexation of Canada which no one seriously suggests today. Even as late as the twentieth century ebullient statements of "manifest destiny," uttered by officials in the United States, aroused violent nationalistic reactions north of the border. In Latin America "Yankee imperialism" was a fighting phrase for many years. The modern world, however, is not seriously troubled by the inferences involved in those words.

In addition to dropping expansionist ideas in this hemisphere, we restricted the scope of our commitments in the Far East. When the Philippines were promised their independence, it was a clear gesture of retirement from our most explicit and onerous obligation in the western Pacific. The Washington Conference of 1921–22 resulted not merely in a reduction of our potential power in the western Pacific; it also involved a reduction of our Far Eastern commitments. We recognized that in renouncing the right to build new fortifications west of Hawaii, we were yielding to Japan a dominant position in that region. We believed, however, that the termination of the Anglo-Japanese alliance of 1902 and the union of other powers with Pacific interests in a common treaty would pool their responsibilities. It was hoped, moreover, and not without reason, that Japan, having no grounds to feel itself cornered, might become a cooperative member of international society.

Those hopes came measurably close to fulfillment. Their failure was not the result of our yielding naval dominance in the western Pacific; to have attempted to maintain it would have been to undertake expenditures and to suggest imperialistic aims which those who now criticize our weakness would not then have supported. On that point the record is clear; no important naval bases which Congress and American public opinion were ready to build were renounced by the Washington Conference; appropriations

85

for further fortification could not be secured even after Japan abrogated the treaty.

The failure of the policy arose from the ensuing disintegration of the political structure of the world. When the peace-loving states failed to work together, those with a tendency to be warlike were encouraged to break loose from the comity of nations. Without that sound international structure, any attempt on our part to maintain naval domination in the western Pacific would merely have precipitated a war with Japan earlier—and it might have been fought without the support of other countries, which we now have.

Chapter XI

CANADA AND GREENLAND

"In talking about foreign policy it is well to remember, as Justice Holmes said, that a page of history is worth a volume of logic." Secretary Hull was seeking, by those words, to correct a false perspective. An understanding of the historical setting of each commitment in American foreign policy helps to offset the difficulties characteristic of our time. Origin and development explain the present and, to some extent, forecast the future. Historical perspective is a necessary corrective of geopolitical dogma. The flow of events is fully as vital as the physical facts; occurrences in time are as real as rocks and rivers in space.

Canada, our immediate neighbor, offers a natural starting point. Its boundary, our longest, is largely undefended. Even before Poland was invaded in 1939, precipitating the armed struggle in Europe, President Roosevelt said explicitly that the Dominion could not be attacked without drawing the United States into war. Critics of the statement argued that it was extraordinary doctrine that Canada could declare war and send troops to fight a European country without protest from the United States, whereas if, in the course of that war, the Dominion itself were invaded, we would fly to its defense. The thesis was described by some in such terms that we appeared to have surrendered to Canada the determination of our policy with regard to peace and war. When we view that commitment in perspective, however, it takes on a different color; the President's speech at Kingston, Ontario, on August 18, 1938, was the inevitable climax of a long historical development.

On the morrow of the American Revolution, when Canada remained a colony of Great Britain, George Washington perceived that there would inevitably be a special relationship between that country and the United States. He was the first to suggest that the Great Lakes be neutralized. In instructions for the famous mission of Chief Justice John Jay to Great Britain to liquidate questions remaining after the Revolution, Washington definitely proposed that "in peace no troops be kept within a limited distance of the Lakes." Jay, however, could not secure an agreement to that effect.

Since the Lakes, the trade dependent upon them, and the Indians whose highways they constituted remained in British hands, the failure of the proposal made many believe that Canada must be acquired. This conviction was exploited by the War Hawks who helped produce the War of 1812 in the hope of conquering Canada. Though the peace treaty did not mention the matter, one result of that war, not then fully appreciated, was the end of British domination on the Lakes. With the loss of that dominance came the loss of British control of the Indians and the trade.

The growing realization that competing navies on the Lakes would prove costly and increase the risk of another war resulted in the celebrated Rush-Bagot Agreement, strictly limiting naval forces. Signed in 1817, this agreement was the fruit of negotiations which were substantially continuous after 1814. It effectively established an open border which the United States has come to regard as a virtual guarantee of peace with Canada. But it had very much larger implications. It meant that whenever Canada, voluntarily or otherwise, might become a base of operations against the United States, we must choose between establishing our defense line beyond the Dominion and in that manner keeping the war away from our borders, or fortifying a long, strategically impossible boundary, while inviting the enemy to develop bases within striking distance of our country.

As long as Britain was regarded as a potential, or even likely, aggressor, we needed to be in a position to outflank Canada. When other nations loomed as possible enemies, it was still essential to include Canada within our defense system. Its population has never been more than a fraction of our own. It could not meet a strong invader without aid, and if at any time the British navy lost control of the North Atlantic, the Dominion would be vulnerable. Under such circumstances our choice of policy in favor of defending Canada was inevitable.

This was the historical basis of the President's assurance in 1938 that "the people of the United States will not stand idly by if the domination of Canadian soil is threatened by any other empire." He was merely stating in explicit terms what had long been our implicit policy. From this policy the United States has had rich dividends. Not only have there been relative security and peace for over a century and a quarter between the United States and its northern neighbor, with all that involves in economy, but Canada has been in a position to serve as a buffer between us and invasion. If, as nations moved into this conflict, there appeared to be a temporary assessment rather than a regular dividend, if for the moment our commitment regarding Canada involved higher costs, there is no reason to regret a policy which time has proved to be fundamentally sound. Perspective upon it reveals that it unites economy with security.

We have defined Greenland as part of the North American Continent and placed it within our defense line. This action is closely related to our policy regarding Canada; the history of the commitment is by no means so long, but neither is it of recent origin.

The experience of the United States in the Civil War led Secretary of State Seward to an appreciation of the presuppositions of sea power. Recognizing the need for bases off our coasts, he not only sought outposts in the Pacific and the Caribbean but he also considered the desirability of acquiring Greenland and possibly Iceland. At his request, one of his confidential advisers presented an exhaustive report in 1868, which discussed the advantages involved in the purchase of Greenland.

The immediate circumstances in which the report was written laid the emphasis upon securing Greenland not as a base for the defense of Canada and the United States, but because it outflanked Canada. The unfriendly disposition of the British Government during the Civil War had produced serious tensions. Early in 1861 Seward had considered war with Great Britain; a little later Britain had joined the European forces that landed in Mexico; and in 1863 our Minister in London had used the phrase "this is war" in regard to the impending departure of one of the Laird rams. Danger of war with Britain, therefore, seemed very real. In such a war Britain might use Canada for a base of operations as it had in 1812. Seward sought, by acquiring Greenland, to prevent any such strategy in the future. He hoped, by outflanking Canada, to induce that colony "peacefully and cheerfully to become a part of the American Union." Precisely the same argument was used to justify the annexation of Alaska which outflanks Canada on the west as Greenland does on the east. The Alaskan purchase was completed but the Greenland project fell through.

This episode shows that whenever the defense of our northern states becomes an acute issue, a renewal of concern about Greenland is inevitable. The historical facts also demonstrate a serious defect in geopolitical dogmas. Within the rigid framework of the same geographical "realities" and even within a relatively fixed pattern of strategic concepts, there occurred a complete reversal of policy. From being conceived as a checkmate upon Canada and explicitly designed to impair or destroy her independence, the North Atlantic extension of the American defense zone has become a bulwark of her integrity. Thus while the tangibles remained unchanged, the intangibles altered in a revolutionary manner. Instead of geography determining policy, policy merely exploited geographical circumstances.

Chapter XII

THE CARIBBEAN

THE United States has a profound interest in the Caribbean, which, from a naval point of view, has become virtually an American lake. Like the commitment in the north with respect to Canada, there is a long and important history behind that fact. Even before we possessed Florida and Texas the strategic significance, both military and political, of the Caribbean was amply clear to American statesmen. They were determined to have Florida and they anticipated the annexation of Cuba.

As early as 1810 President Madison said: "The position of Cuba gives the United States so deep an interest in the destiny . . . of that island that although they might be an inactive, they could not be a satisfied spectator at its falling under any European government which might make a fulcrum of that position against the commerce and security of the United States." As time went on successive government officials made stronger statements. John Quincy Adams summed up the whole matter in 1823 when he instructed the new Minister to the Court of Madrid: "In looking forward to the probable course of events for the short period of half a century, it seems scarcely possible to resist the conviction that the annexation of Cuba to our Federal Republic will be indispensable to the continuance and integrity of the Union itself."

The upshot of that policy was the Spanish-American

War, but not the long expected annexation of Cuba. On the contrary, the independence of the island was recognized although the United States retained military control, an important naval base, and political leadership. As time passed and the military position of the United States became overwhelmingly strong in the region, political control over Cuba was relaxed and the relationship between the two nations liberalized. It remains true, however, that if any foreign power were to attempt to use the island in a manner which imperiled the United States, its vital strategic importance would again be revealed. It is also true that for strategic reasons Cuba is in some respects dependent upon the United States. The scope for Cuban political action is trammeled by those basic facts.

Similar considerations govern our relationship to other areas in the Caribbean. A few years before the Civil War the United States negotiated unsuccessfully for a coaling station at Samana Bay in Santo Domingo. Events in that war demonstrated anew not only the need for such a station but the difficulty in preventing blockade runners, based on the British and French islands, from reaching Southern ports. Consequently, during the war we leased St. Nicholas Bay in Haiti. After the war President Grant wanted to annex the Dominican Republic; this action was prevented in the Senate by a narrow margin. Under the administration of Theodore Roosevelt we took a position of economic and political dominance, partly to prevent possible interference by European powers. During the First World War, the United States actively intervened in Haiti and the Dominican Republic and virtually occupied the whole island. There has been no such gesture in this war, because, both in a strategic and a political sense, it has become needless. The controlling position of the United States has made leadership and cooperation an adequate substitute.

The Civil War revealed the strategic importance of the Virgin Islands, then in the possession of Denmark. Admiral Porter stated that St. Thomas was a potential Gibraltar, central, defensible, and desirable from every point of view. Seward's effort to buy the archipelago failed by an even narrower margin than President Grant's attempt to take over the larger island of Santo Domingo. The Spanish-American War raised the issue anew, and negotiations for purchase were again attempted, but broke down. With the First World War, the possibility that Germany might acquire the Danish islands brought the matter of control once more to the front, and they were purchased in 1917.

It is a significant fact, altogether too little appreciated, that since the Monroe Doctrine Great Britain has developed no important naval bases in Bermuda, the Bahamas, Jamaica, other islands in the Caribbean, or British Guiana. This was not a consequence of any agreement, expressed or even tacitly implied, between the United States and Britain. Indeed through much of the nineteenth century there was keen rivalry which occasionally threatened to lead to hostilities. Tensions during the Civil War and again in the administration of President Cleveland were conclusive evidence that no agreement existed.

The reason Britain did not construct important naval bases in the northern half of this hemisphere was that United States policy was so clear and so firm that it did not pay to offer so direct a provocation to trouble. Our interest was so dominant that to challenge it directly meant rivalries in armaments and possibly war. The present World War has brought the matter to its inevitable historical climax. As these potential bases became less valuable to Britain, the airplane extended our defense perimeter. The exchange of destroyers in 1940 for leased areas available for advanced bases for the United States was simply a logical culmination of a long series of events. Strategic realities were recognized without transfer of sovereignty or a change in the political institutions and the loyalty of the inhabitants.

The history of the Panama Canal reveals a similar development of American policy in the Caribbean. The need for a canal was evident as soon as California was acquired, but Britain had interests of such strength that we could not then extinguish them. In 1850 the Clayton-Bulwer Treaty recognized that the free hand of the United States was limited; this recognition was not due to inept diplomacy; it merely reflected the historical realities of the situation. These facts were not palatable, and for fifty years thereafter our determination to control the canal continued to grow. Both the desire and the basis for it were stated with perfect explicitness by President Hayes in 1880: "The policy of this country is a canal under American control. . . . An inter-oceanic canal across the American Isthmus will essentially change the geographical relations between the Atlantic and Pacific coasts of the United States. . . . It would be the great ocean thoroughfare between our . . . shores, and *virtually a part of the coast line of the United States*." (Italics supplied.)

The pace by which the Hayes doctrine was brought into the scope of action was hastened by the Spanish-American War and the dramatic race of the "Oregon" around South America. The passage of that battleship gave the American people a great object lesson in the strategic significance of the canal. It caught their imagination, revealing

95

that we must promptly double our navy or cut a canal.

The episode fortunately coincided with an era of cordial feeling between the United States and Great Britain. The fundamental reorientation of attitude between those countries at the end of the nineteenth century has fairly been called a diplomatic revolution. Although there have been serious differences and many irritations since that time, the basic relationships between the two nations have been not only friendly, but, on the whole, cooperative.

The canal policy enunciated by Hayes with such crystal clarity was implemented by the Hay-Pauncefote Treaty whereby Britain substantially retired in favor of the United States. Panama then became independent with our connivance, the zone was acquired, and the canal constructed.

From that moment military dominance has become more and more complete. The power basis for an imperialistic policy was fully established. We were in a position to work our will. The rejection of power politics as the key to our actions is dramatically revealed by the fact that political relationships within the region have been expressed more in terms of mutual interest, more in phrases of cooperation, and less in accents of domination. The reality that American military policy controls the Caribbean as part of our coastline, however, is fully understood and is unchallenged.

Chapter XIII

SOUTH AMERICA

THE South American policy of the United States has grown slowly. Its origins antedated the Monroe Doctrine by many years. As Spanish Americans broke away from Bourbon control, their efforts toward freedom and independence were stimulated by the United States. The trend from monarchy toward republicanism also engaged the moral support of this country. The instructions to our first diplomatic agent in South America, in 1810, declared that "the geographical position of the United States and other obvious considerations give them an intimate interest in whatever may affect the destiny of that part of the American continent."

The Monroe Doctrine was a dramatic episode in the continuing interest. In the 1820's it looked as though an effort might be made to restore South America to Spain. The President of the United States gave expression to this nation's concern. The sentence which is significant follows: "We could not view any interposition for the purpose of oppressing them or controlling in any other manner their destiny by any European power in any other light than as the manifestation of an unfriendly disposition toward the United States." Those words do not contain a threat to fight anyone who "violated" the doctrine, although they are often so interpreted and in that way the nature of our commitment is overstated. During periods of ardent self-

97

consciousness and occasionally when imperialism or other influences made bumptiousness seem good tactics, our claims have been more sweeping. But the essential policy so clearly enunciated in 1823 remains undisturbed.

The declaration was based upon no understanding with Britain. John Quincy Adams, the dominant figure in its promulgation, rejected the joint basis which appealed to Jefferson and Madison. He wanted an independent expression of American interest; he was determined we should go it alone and not come in like "a cockboat in the wake of the British man-of-war." Therefore, while George Canning boasted that he "called the New World into existence to redress the balance of the Old," Adams recognized more clearly than some modern commentators that the phrase came closer to political bombast than a description of what really happened.

The Monroe Doctrine was not founded upon any assertion or even any assumption that the states of America were, or would become, democracies. It described them with meticulous accuracy as "the governments who have declared their independence and maintained it." It spoke of the political system of the allied powers as being essentially different; that also was precisely accurate. When one remembers that the statement referred to the Europe of the Bourbons and Hapsburgs, monarchies based upon the principle of "legitimacy," the distinction between that political system and the emerging revolutionary republicanism of this hemisphere was adequately clear.

It is, therefore, no stain upon the Monroe Doctrine and no evidence of its "failure" that the nations of Latin America are not all democracies. The policy of the United States made this hemisphere, in the classic phrase of Woodrow

Wilson, "safe for democracy." We have done much to encourage republican government on a democratic basis in the nations to the south; it was never our intention to force democracy down their throats. If we are as wise as our forefathers, we shall be satisfied to continue stimulating the development of free institutions. They were never so short-sighted as to suppose that freedom could be extemporized; we should have neither less faith nor more pessimism than they.

It should be observed, moreover, that our policy has been realistic in regard to South America. As events during this war make clear, our relationship with Argentina is not the same as our relationship with Brazil, and those relationships reflect, among other things, strategic differences. It is a conspicuous fact that whereas Great Britain did not develop naval bases anywhere in the Northern Hemisphere, we acquiesced in British possession of the Falkland Islands after the enunciation of the Monroe Doctrine, and they have been employed as a base for naval operations without protest by the United States.

As the American political system has matured, and the threat of European domination by force has been effectively removed, there has been a greater and greater tendency to regard the Monroe Doctrine not as a shibboleth of the United States alone, but as an expression of hemispheric policy. This accounts for what has often been called the mutualization of the doctrine under the leadership of Secretary Hull. A striking illustration was the Act of Havana, unanimously approved by the representatives of the American Republics, July 30, 1940. In view of "the grave danger that European territorial possessions in America may be converted into strategic centers of aggression against nations of the American continent," the act provided "that when islands or regions in the Americas now under the possession of non-American nations are in danger of becoming the subject of barter of territory or change of sovereignty, the American nations . . . may set up a regime of provisional administration." It stipulated that "as soon as the reasons requiring this measure shall cease to exist . . . such territories shall . . . be organized as autonomous States . . . or be restored to their previous status, whichever of these alternatives shall appear the more practicable and just."

This "continentalization" of the Monroe Doctrine was not the result of weakness upon the part of the United States. It was a recognition that the original purposes of our unilateral declaration had been substantially achieved; the interests of all American states on this point were mutual. It was evidence that the leadership of the United States was well enough established so that we need no longer "go it alone."

The substance of the Monroe policy remains; American interest is the same; the only change is a recognition of the altered status of the nations of the Southern Hemisphere. Modern expressions of our policy are still realistic, but phrased with more urbanity. Such bombastic outbursts as that of Secretary Olney in 1895, when he said that our "fiat is law," would not now be tolerated by American opinion. Nonetheless, the United States continues to exercise real leadership within the hemisphere.

Achievement of our desires has come to depend more upon reason than pressure. Our recognition policy has returned almost to its classic "de facto" basis. We ask only that the new government be in effective control, and that it give evidence of its readiness to fulfill its international obligations. The recent refusal to recognize the government of Argentina rests not upon its revolutionary character, but upon its failure to discharge the obligations regarding hemispheric defense which it had assumed in company with the other American nations. We no longer exert leverage upon the internal affairs of Latin nations by insisting upon constitutional legitimacy as in the days of Woodrow Wilson. Their freedom to order their politics as they choose is appreciated. United States marines no longer occupy any of the republics of Central America; the collection of private debts and claims involves diplomacy with no threat of force. It is no idle boast that both the use of force and the show of force have come to play very minor roles in inter-American relationships. Realizing the cultural barriers, the United States is making extraordinary efforts to achieve mutual understanding; the attitude of superiority has given way to appreciation. Economic activities are often competitive, but something is being done to accentuate common interests.

CHAPTER XIV

THE PACIFIC

THE historical character of American commitments is revealed again in the Pacific region. Before the expanding boundaries of the United States reached the coast, steps were taken to prevent Russia from consolidating its hold in this hemisphere. John Quincy Adams as Secretary of State for President Monroe specifically told the Russian Minister, Baron Tuyl, that "we should contest the right of Russia to any territorial establishment on this continent, and that we should assume distinctly the principle that the American continents are no longer subjects for any new European colonial establishments." It was the North American part of the Monroe Doctrine.

During the following decades our interests steadily expanded. Before going to Japan Matthew Calbraith Perry wrote a memorandum which summarized our viewpoint:

"The tide of empire is gradually flowing westward, and for the next half-century the most prominent events of the world are to transpire in the Western Hemisphere, and especially in the Pacific Ocean. From the geographical position of the United States, and their rapidly growing commerce between the shores of the Pacific and China, and the Polynesian Islands, our people must naturally be drawn into the contest for empire, whether for good or for evil, and it will be wise to anticipate and prepare for events inevitable in themselves."

Seward echoed Perry's doctrine when he said:

"The Pacific Ocean, its shores, its islands, and the vast regions beyond will become the chief theatre of events in the world's great hereafter."

He frequently declared that the Union should extend from the North Pole to the tropics:

"Our population is destined to roll its resistless waves to the icy barriers of the North and to encounter oriental civilization on the shores of the Pacific."

It was partly under this impulse that Seward negotiated the purchase of Alaska and the Aleutian Islands. The project was not new. Secretary Marcy had proposed the purchase, and in 1859 definite overtures were made on behalf of President Buchanan. When the Civil War proved as decisive in calling attention to Pacific strategy as to Atlantic, Seward took advantage of the groundwork which had been laid. His achievement was a triumph of secrecy, swiftness, and suavity. Amidst all the sarcasm and ridicule heaped upon the transaction, he pursued his way with vigor and success.

Among other reasons for the acquisition, he argued that it would flank Canada; he hoped thereby to induce the Dominion to become part of the American Union. In fact the United States only gradually relinquished this ambition. It virtually flickered out with the development of good feeling between the United States and Great Britain which has so far characterized the twentieth century. In the mid-nineteenth century relations were far less cordial, and the Alaskan purchase was influenced by that fact. Even Russia favored the transfer, in part, because it would discomfit Britain. The Russian Minister felt "the conquest of California by the Yankees was the first effective blow to Great

Britain's ambitions in the Pacific, and the acquisition of Alaska would put an end to them altogether." Under changed political circumstances, the extension of our defense zone in the northwest has become a protection to Canada, instead of a threat.

Our commitment regarding Hawaii is even older. As early as 1818 the United States was interested in the islands, and a diplomatic agent expressed apprehension lest they fall under control of the Russians. Eight years later our representative negotiated a treaty of friendship and commerce. It soon became part of our program to keep Hawaii out of the hands of the British and the French, as well as the Russians.

Secretary of State Webster defined our position in 1842:

"The United States . . . are more interested in the fate of the islands and of their Government than any other nation can be; and this consideration induces the President to be quite willing to declare, as the sense of the Government of the United States, that the Government of the Sandwich Islands ought to be respected; that no power ought either to take possession of the islands as a conquest or for the purpose of colonization and that no power ought to seek for any undue control over the existing Government, or any exclusive privileges or preferences with it in matters of commerce."

This was an early expression of American interest in the "open door" and the integrity of nations threatened with exploitation or spoliation.

In June 1843, the *ad interim* Secretary of State wrote to our Minister in London that "the United States might feel justified in interfering by force to prevent Hawaii falling, by conquest, into the hands of one of the great powers of

Europe." In the same year Britain and France agreed to regard the islands as independent and never to take possession of them either directly or indirectly.

Thereafter the settlement of the Oregon dispute and the California Gold Rush increased our concern in the Pacific. In 1849 Secretary of State Clayton, though he had recognized a British interest in the Isthmian Canal through the Clayton-Bulwer Treaty, nevertheless took a strong position in relation to the Hawaiian Islands, notifying our Minister in Paris that "the United States could never with indifference allow them to pass under the dominion or exclusive control of any other power."

Two years later, in pursuance of this policy, the Navy Department was instructed to keep a sufficient force in the Pacific "for the preservation of the honor and dignity of the United States and the safety of the government of Hawaii." Lord Palmerston, the British Foreign Secretary, had predicted that the islands would eventually come to America. At the close of the decade we laid claim to Midway, one of the Leeward Islands of the Hawaiian Archipelago, taking possession in 1867.

With this background it was natural that Seward should see the strategic necessity for the acquisition of Hawaii. In discussing a pending reciprocity treaty he declared that "a lawful and peaceful annexation of the islands to the United States, with the consent of the people of the Sandwich Islands, is deemed desirable by this Government; . . . if the policy of annexation should really conflict with the policy of reciprocity, annexation is in every case to be preferred." Lack of popular interest in the measure led him to remark that "we have come to value dollars more and dominion less." Within a few years, however, a

105

reciprocity treaty proved acceptable and trade increased enormously. Economic benefits began to have the significance which strategic considerations had suggested. Furthermore missionaries had built up a religious tie which grew in political importance.

Under President Garfield a new factor appeared. The danger that the Japanese might take an interest in the archipelago, to which many of their citizens had been transported as laborers, led to the declaration that "the Hawaiian Islands cannot be joined to the Asiatic system." Successive efforts upon the part of Great Britain to break through the American policy were likewise steadily resisted, even by administrations which were far from imperialistic.

By 1887 the United States had acquired the exclusive right to enter Pearl Harbor and to establish a coaling and naval repair station there. But when events in Hawaii resulted in a treaty of annexation late in the Harrison administration, it was withdrawn by President Cleveland. Later a new treaty, negotiated in 1897, was not acted on by the Senate. It had aroused foreign opposition led by Japan, which already had the largest single element in the population, almost four times as large a percentage as the American. Great Britain also objected. However, the Spanish-American War with its naval operations in the Far East demonstrated the necessity of our possessing Hawaii for strategic reasons, and it was annexed by joint resolution on July 7, 1898.

The Hawaiian episode is offered as a typical illustration of the development of national policy. We sought an "open door" and an independent state; we resisted interference by Russia, Great Britain, and France. Failure in the effort to keep a native state independent resulted in annexation and a clash of interests with Japan which ultimately came to its denouement on December 7, 1941, with the attack on Pearl Harbor, a culmination foreseen as a possibility sixty years before.

The interest of the United States in the Samoan Islands goes back before the Civil War; then the broad naval strategy of Seward was bound to include the South Pacific. It is significant that it was an American naval officer who first, without authority, made a treaty in 1872 giving the United States the right to a naval base at Pago Pago. The Senate did not approve the treaty, but the State Department from that time forward adopted the policy of keeping other nations from taking Samoa. In 1878, by treaty, we acquired exclusive rights for a coaling and naval station. The Germans, however, followed a policy of gradual infiltration and seemed much tempted to seize the islands. This produced friction which almost culminated in a naval engagement in 1889, when hostilities were forestalled by a hurricane that destroyed both squadrons. By the logic of the acquisition of Hawaii and the Philippines, Samoa became the southern anchor of our long outpost defense lines. The treaty of 1899, superseding joint supervision by Great Britain, Germany, and the United States, divided the islands between the two last powers. After the First World War the German possessions became a mandate of New Zealand.

The acquisition of the Philippines, Guam, and Wake belongs in the realm of historical accident. The United States had no special interest in the islands and little knowledge of them. The war with Spain had no necessary relationship to the Philippines, but on the principle of fighting the enemy wherever he was to be found, a naval battle occurred at Manila Bay. It proved a decisive engagement without the loss of a single American life. The victory was so sensational that it was difficult to give up its tangible fruits. President McKinley summarized the situation in his instructions to the commissioners who negotiated peace: "Without any original thought of complete or even partial acquisition, the presence and success of our arms at Manila impose upon us obligations which we cannot disregard."

These events coincided with the popular absorption of the ideas of Admiral Mahan regarding the importance of sea power, and fell into the pattern of a vast wave of imperialism which swept not only the United States but the world. In that era a great many rivalries for position in international politics were liquidated by partition. Spain was obviously on the way out of the Far East. It was certain that if we failed to take the Philippines, some European nation would annex them. Germany had acquired the Marshall Islands in 1885 and four years later purchased from Spain the Mariannes or Ladrones (except Guam), the Carolines, and the Palau Islands.

Following the First World War all the German islands in the Pacific were ceded to the five principal Allied and Associated Powers. On the basis of an agreement between Britain and Japan, concluded before our entry into the war, the islands north of the equator were mandated to Japan, those south to Australia and New Zealand. The United States effectively insisted upon its ownership of a one-fifth undivided interest, but did not block the mandates; nor did it insist that Japan obey in letter and spirit the terms of the mandate. This was one more evidence of a determination to retire to a defense line based on Pearl Harbor, and to depend upon international cooperation to preserve peace in the western Pacific. The Nine-Power Treaty of the Washington Conference, signed February 6, 1922, was designed for that purpose.

The United States took the Philippines from a mixture of excitement, pride, missionary zeal, imperialism, and a desire to prevent some other nation from doing it. Disillusionment followed the Philippine rebellion, however; the political missionary spirit waned; the economy of the islands became seriously competitive; the Washington Conference made their strategic position essentially untenable. All these factors dictated a reversal of the decision of 1898 and led to preparations for retirement.

CHAPTER XV

THE FAR EAST

INTEREST in the Far East belongs in a wholly different
category from that in the Philippines. It was neither accidental nor imperialistic, but old and well settled. At an
early date the United States endeavored to negotiate treaties
with the islands of the Far East and with the various sul-
tans, rajas, and princes on the continent in order to facilitate trade and assist our whalers. In 1832 an envoy was
instructed to inform these powers that "we never make
conquests, or ask any nations to let us establish ourselves
in their country as the English, the French, and the Dutch
have done in the East Indies." That statement had the
essence of the "open door" policy, and it also expressed
the concept of the integrity of native states.

The United States was among the first to make a treaty
with China, but its boldest and most decisive commitment
was the expedition of Commodore Perry in 1854, when he
insisted upon the opening of Japan and used the threat of
force to achieve it. The interest was basically commercial.
Although the policy of the "open door" in China was
dramatized by John Hay in 1899, he merely summarized
and made explicit the fundamental principle of our relations with the Far East. The accompanying policy of the
integrity of China was expressed in more restricted terms
in regard to Japan because the latter was never menaced
with disintegration.

Early commitments in the Far East dealt with old civilizations which were retarded politically. The nature of our relationship with the nations of the East was defined before they entered world politics, while their military power was negligible and naval power nonexistent. Diplomatic arguments were supplemented by threats of force from time to time and even by the use of force. Because force was employed upon a small scale and brought quick results, those episodes have largely been forgotten by us, but not by the orientals.

The program of the United States always contained the possibility of friction with Japan after that nation entered upon its modern development. The potentialities for trouble-making upon the part of Japan would have been vastly increased by the Anglo-Japanese alliance of 1902 but for the fact that an era of good feeling between the United States and Great Britain coincided with the period of the alliance. The First World War and its results made it clear that Britain must choose between its friends. Two nations of the British Commonwealth, Australia and Canada, were opposed to the Anglo-Japanese alliance. So, in the effort to liquidate the problems of the Far East at the Washington Conference of 1921–22, the compact was terminated. The wonder is not that we are now at war with Japan; a triumph of diplomacy and of skill staved off the war for many years and brought us to the struggle as the ally of the other great naval power.

Nothing is clearer than that American commitments in the Far East were markedly reduced during the past twenty years. The Washington Conference deliberately left naval predominance in the western Pacific with Japan. The move for the independence of the Philippines highlighted our withdrawal. The Stimson doctrine of non-recognition, stated in the note of January 7, 1932, to both Japan and China, obviously represented dependence upon moral and political pressure rather than force. Our strategic line of defense was the Alaska, Hawaii, Samoa line; Wake and Guam were mere outposts designed for peace rather than for war.

What the future policy of the United States will be depends upon the outcome of the present war—not only the victory over Japan, but the effect of the war and the peace upon China and its integrity, upon the Soviet Union and its aggressiveness or cooperation, upon the colonial status of the Netherland Indies, of Burma, Malaya, French Indo-China, and the position of Siam and Korea. On many of these matters the United States will exert a profound influence; on others the essential decisions will rest elsewhere, particularly with the Soviet Union and China. There is little likelihood that the former Spanish and German archipelagoes will be left in the hands of Japan, to become at some future time a spearhead against us. It may well be, also, that in order to ensure the redemption of the Philippines from the Japanese we shall maintain a larger power position in the western Pacific as reinsurance of international collaboration.

CHAPTER XVI

EUROPE

IN contrast with its relationship to the Far East, the United States was for 150 years a dependency of Europe. In the eighteenth century, war in Europe regularly meant war in America; even in the early nineteenth century, European machinations threatened, and actually produced, embroilment. The War of American Independence was itself part of a European struggle; its conclusion did not alter the basic European rivalries. The whole Western Hemisphere, except for the limited space allotted to the United States, was still in European hands—and actively within the orbit of European politics.

The history of involvement for many years in many wars as a pawn of imperialist nations taught a lesson. If human experience has any fruits in wisdom, that was inevitable. After struggling in a long and exhausting war to break loose physically, the United States for many years sought by diplomatic and commercial means to achieve a real independence economically, morally, and politically. Its history until the administration of James Monroe records a continuous effort to escape from Europe and European commitments.

So long as Napoleon lived no nation, however remote, could feel safe. Even after Napoleon was gone, the ensuing peace was based upon premises hostile to our national life. "Legitimacy," the denial and suppression of revolutionary action; power politics; alliances; all these belonged to a system antithetical to our own. Safety lay in an "American system," in developing internal resources, in expanding our borders, in exploiting the defensive possibilities inherent in the breadth of the Atlantic Ocean, in stimulating colonial revolt and separatism, in spreading the infection of our peculiar institutions.

Washington was strictly accurate when he asserted that "Europe has a set of primary interests which to us have none or a very remote relation." Monroe was not at all extravagant in looking upon attempts to control any part of this hemisphere from another as dangerous to our peace and safety. To our ears Webster sounds arrogant in his assertion to the Austrian Chargé: "The power of this republic, at the present moment, is spread over a region, one of the richest and most fertile upon the globe, and of an extent in comparison with which the possessions of the House of Hapsburg are but a patch upon the earth's surface." However, it was the normal response of a warm-blooded American to a bearing of supercilious superiority, to the more subtle, but nonetheless real, arrogance of the decaying Hapsburgs.

Certainly imperialism did not die with Napoleon. The British Empire, after the setback of 1783, continued to grow steadily. This was both cause and effect of its dominance as a sea power—each additional possession enlarged imperial strategy and necessitated a more powerful Royal Navy. At the same time Russia pushed southward into the Caucasus and central Asia and put forward its energies in eastern Asia until it was an important Pacific power.

During the last quarter of the nineteenth century this imperialism went wild. France seized lands in Indo-China

114

and Africa until its colonies surpassed in size and potential resources those it had lost in the eighteenth century. Germany, despite the lukewarmness of Bismarck, grasped territory in Africa, bought Pacific islands, acquired concessions in China, and showed the aggressive spirit that ultimately precipitated war. Even the King of the Belgians staked out a vast claim in the Congo Free State. Japan, imitating the West, substituted expansion for isolation; wars with China and Russia gave evidence of the nature and extent of its ambitions.

In the midst of this virulent global infection the remarkable fact is that the United States showed such high resistance. It acquired nothing outside its historic zone and strategic area save the Philippines; it sought to protect China from being carved up; it refused to annex Cuba. If Olney's tone to Britain in the Venezuela boundary dispute was sharp, it was because aggression everywhere found its cloak in what began as minor incidents; by vindicating the Monroe Doctrine with such vigor, and even violence, he put all nations on notice. As a new world power the United States could easily have entered the scramble for territory; it is one of the valuable consequences of the isolationist tradition that it did not.

The basic foreign policy of America was negative, as its basic strategy was defensive. It pioneered in the quarantine of war by developing early in its history the concept of neutrality—the right of a non-belligerent to its own life. A distinguished authority on international law epitomized its importance: "The policy of the United States in 1793 constitutes an epoch in the development of the usages of neutrality." Is it any wonder that a concept which proved so valuable should be tenaciously held? It was natural,

115

for the same reasons, that this country should center its energies upon the pacific settlement of disputes by mediation, arbitration, and the judicial process. From the Jay Treaty of 1794 through the Second Hague Conference of 1907, the United States led the other nations in these fields. It is fashionable, momentarily, to discount moral leadership under the falsely "realistic" assumption that power is all that counts. Cynics point out that our moral views coincided with our interests. They do not make clear that our interest in peace did not run counter to world interest. The happy coincidence of national and world peace with moral positions should not be shrugged off so easily.

For much of our history there was no inconsistency between moral leadership and political isolationism. The ideas and attitudes we could contribute were more potent than our manpower or productive capacity. That these circumstances did not acquire permanence is no argument against their validity for the appropriate era. The basis for an isolationist policy was destroyed when imperialism had engrossed all available territory and the United States had become a world power. Our strategic location, our growing war potential, and our dominance in the Western Hemisphere could not fail to have profound effects. In the primary problem of universal peace we were as deeply involved as Europe or Asia. John Hay, Theodore Roosevelt, Elihu Root, and others saw this and participated in events, such as the Algeciras Conference, which were primarily European.

The changed political structure of the world, together with modern communication and transport, had altered our traditional position. We no longer occupied, as in

Washington's day, a "detached and distant situation." We no longer had to "quit our own to stand on foreign ground." That lesson was learned between 1914 and 1917; it seems incredible that it should ever have been forgotten. But the fact is plain, and reminds us that policy does not reflect geography or current situations only; it is rooted in the past and to some extent dominated by the past. Experience, emotion, momentum are parts of it—and revolutionary changes of policy are likely to bring reaction.

Now the lesson is being learned again. Many say that this time it will not be forgotten. Of that we cannot be sure. Some are overlooking a still older lesson, and suggest, as a basic policy, "passionate attachments" and "inveterate antipathies"—two attitudes against which, on the basis of experience, Washington warned. Such a proposal neglects, among other things, the fact that Japan and Italy were our allies in the last war. It disregards the probability that political shifts, changed social situations, fresh cultural developments will bring to a dominant position men who have long been overwhelmed. Our task is to encourage and stimulate the control of policy by leaders who have an outlook upon the world similar to our own.

Holding a whole nation in permanent subjection is a futile enterprise. The solution cannot be so simple. We must participate in world affairs, "as our interest, guided by justice, shall counsel." That can never mean complete freedom of action; there is not enough elbow-room left in the world. We cannot run away; there is no place to run. We cannot retire within ourselves; autarchy brings war. There is no simple formula for our relationship to all the rest of the world. We ought, however, to maintain our far-flung bases. Then, "taking care always to keep ourselves by suitable establishments on a respectable defensive posture, we may safely trust to temporary alliances for extraordinary emergencies."

That program is one of reinsurance while a world political structure develops. In the immediate future, functional agencies of international life will exist in great numbers; we should participate fully and unreservedly in all in which we have a genuine interest, and which follow a pattern in harmony with our political ideals. They will be judicial, scientific, technical, economic, social. All will have political implications, and from those we should no longer shrink. We should strive to coordinate the many agencies into a single structure. In due time it might become a world government; ultimately a "parliament of man" might develop. Haste to go too far, too fast, will provoke reaction. Progress in the right direction is more important than speed in any direction.

Our relationships with the British Commonwealth are of vital importance. They have all the strengths and weaknesses of intimacy. Just as families have strong bonds, and all too frequent quarrels, so, historically, our ties with the mother country have followed that pattern. We had two wars with Britain. Boundary difficulties were not only continuous but irritating. Canada, a British connection, frustrated some American imperialists. The behavior of Britain during the Civil War was vexing. A large Irish population in the United States kept alive the antagonisms which grew out of the Irish question. The rivalry for seaborne commerce made the Yankee and the Limey contentious neighbors. When the world was peaceful, we quarreled with Britain, but when the world was dangerous, we drew into cooperation. Even the Francophile Jefferson, the author of the Declaration of Independence, nonetheless threatened to "marry . . . the British fleet and nation" when he distrusted Napoleon's ambition in Louisiana. That fundamental dual orientation appears again and again in our history.

In the twentieth century, the United States, though a world power, and through part of the time with an overweening sense that it was *the* coming world power, pursued its policy of isolation, while Britain pursued a policy of modified isolation. They became makeweights in two balances of power: Britain vis-à-vis Europe and the United States vis-à-vis the world at large. So Britain entered both World Wars to fulfill pledges to small European nations, and the United States came into both wars when a continental power seemed likely to dominate not only central Europe but the shores of Europe and to threaten the sea lanes.

That record gives us our cue. We must learn to cooperate with the British in peace as well as in war, in calm as in tension. Britain cannot pursue an isolationist policy toward Europe, nor we toward world problems. The nations must work to resolve crises while they are minor, rather than when they have reached great magnitude. Munich represented the failure of Britain to follow that policy, and short-sighted neutrality legislation represented our failure. Because we did not grasp the nettle while it was tender, we suffer from it now. The need in the future is for vigor and consistency in meeting problems in their incipient stages; that is, however, one of the most difficult of all political demands, and we can hope only for an approximation.

In that task ideological differences need not prove an insuperable barrier. We have never hidden our own beliefs. We abandoned monarchy and set up a republican form of government. We became the sponsor of republicanism in this hemisphere and the exponent of popular government everywhere in the world. We had early, therefore, a moral commitment to promote and support democracy in Europe. On every occasion we preached that doctrine. Crusty John Quincy Adams recorded in his diary with keen delight that he had read a lecture to the Russian Baron Tuyl on the glories of republicanism and had taken pleasure in annoying the representative of absolutism thereby. Daniel Webster made the eagle scream in his famous letter to Hülsemann in which he declared that the United States cannot "fail to cherish always a lively interest in the fortunes of nations struggling for institutions like our own." This country was alert to recognize revolutionary, and particularly republican, governments and was ostentatiously the haven of refuge for political exiles.

Many instances of the vigorous exposition of our characteristic views could be cited, but they did not prevent fruitful relations with Russia under the Tsars as under the Soviets; we have been friendly or hostile to Spain on various occasions, but the change was not due to similarity or difference in the political views of the two nations; we were an ally of the Bourbon monarchy in France, and then fought the naval war with France after it had adopted "Liberty, Fraternity, Equality" as its slogan. There is no reason we should not hope—and strive—for a democratic world. There is also no reason we should not cooperate in common causes with those who live under different forms of government. We have no occasion to be either apologetic or arrogant; the important requisite is patience. That offers the key to our relationship to the Soviets in the future as it was to our generally friendly contact with the Tsars in the past. We never pretended to admire their despotism; we never sacrificed peace to an ideological fetish. We need not do so in the days to come.

To the impatient contemporary mind, this record may appear to be a case of "muddling through." To those who want to categorize every event and express it in the precise terms of a balance sheet and cautiously determine that there are not more liabilities than assets, this set of commitments may seem difficult to justify. But that doubt is primarily the reflection of a momentary mood of those who forget that we are dealing with forces in time as well as in space, and, even more serious, neglect that we are concerned with an intensely human situation.

If we remember that we are dealing with forces in time, it will be clear that our interests and consequently our commitments have varied over the years, and will continue to do so. Men cannot foresee the future with accuracy. If they could, we should live in a wholly different kind of world. Nor do men assess even the present with precision, for events are too crowded and the panorama too vast. Moreover, public opinion, whether in a dictatorship or a democracy, has some of the elements of a spotlight; it cannot focus upon all subjects at once. Some are in the bright glare and stand out sharply; others are at the margin, only dimly perceived. The adjustment between interests and commitments, therefore, can never be flawless.

The striking characteristic of this record is that over the years and in its large outline American opinion has seen the

121

logic of its position in the world, and from time to time made the adjustments necessary to adapt itself to altered circumstances. If the adaptation on our part and on the part of all the nations had been perfect, there would have been no war. But there is no reason why America should feel that its powers of perception and adjustment, the relationships which it has established between its real interests and its commitments, are more seriously out of balance than those of other nations. There is no reason, either, to expect that by some neat and precise technique such vast forces in a complex environment can ever exactly prepare for unforeseen emergencies. We should strive to do better; there is no need to scold ourselves for not having achieved the ideal.

In its broad outline American foreign policy has been sound. Established as a republic in a world of monarchies, our nation did not take the "realistic" view and conform. With revolutionary courage, we set our own course and undertook to vindicate our unique institutions. In seeking to make this continent safe for our enterprise, we recognized that the New World to the south also needed an opportunity to develop institutions different from those of Europe. And we realized properly that if the institutions were republican, even though not flawless, they would give us a stronger moral position in the world. The Monroe Doctrine, so-called, is one of the oldest foreign policies in the world, and one of the most successful.

In our relationship to the Far East, the "open door" and the integrity of native states are twin policies. They likewise are among the oldest consistently followed by any nation. If other countries had accepted them, the record would be different. In spite of the circumstances and policies of other nations and the enormous pressures upon new territories, those two policies likewise have vindicated themselves.

Until we became a world power and acquired great moral influence, a policy of isolationism toward Europe, never absolute and always relative, was sound. We were less isolationist until Europe, except for British interest in Canada, had been retired from North America, and properly so. When that goal was achieved, when France, Spain, and Russia were banished, isolationism for a nation in process of internal development was essential. But we always stood for freedom to trade, as is shown by our action against the Barbary corsairs and the Danish Sound dues. We were never morally isolated, as our long and vigorous championship of revolutionary and liberal governments demonstrates. We always recognized that the peace was indivisible; consequently we sought to quarantine wars in order to prevent them from spreading and to substitute mediation, arbitration, and judicial settlement for resort to force. In the twentieth century it became necessary to modify the isolationist point of view. That has been done progressively, with alternating periods of advance and reaction, as in all human events.

The incidence of the war has upset many of the conditions which were formerly established. To sit down now and dogmatize about policy without knowledge of what changes the war will bring in social, economic, and political structures the world around is extremely foolish. We must trust to our own wisdom and that of our successors and look to adaptability rather than to fixity for future success.

The only permanent datum in history is change. Geography changes not alone in geologic cycles but by scientific and technological modifications in space relationships and even in the characteristics of terrain. The land masses may be stable; nevertheless man's relationship to them alters from time to time as he spans the ocean, tames the rivers, brings low the mountains, and exalts the valleys.

Man also changes, more slowly indeed than geography. However his ideas and ideals, the institutions which embody them, his moral outlook, and his emotional orientation, all change. They change at different rates, at different times, and in different places; sometimes with great convulsions, such as the Russian Revolution; sometimes by the process of enlightenment; at other times by lapsing into Nazi darkness. Whatever its nature, whatever its pace, and whatever its direction, change is the essence of policy. Consistency may be much worse than the vice of small minds; it may represent failure to adapt oneself to the inevitable.

The record of the United States is part of the fabric of history; it reveals success and failure, partial success and partial failure, moments of brilliant triumph and others of profound defeat. As it has been, it will continue to be. There is nothing in the record to give us hope that there is any substitute for an alert and informed public opinion. We should reject both the dogmas of false scientism in geopolitics and the pessimism of a period of emotional depression. We certainly should not project into the future the confusions of a vast world conflict.

PART III

A BASIC TREATY OF PEACE

UNTIL the spring of 1944 there was a marked contrast between the concrete nature of economic and social phases of post-war planning and the very general character of political preparation for peace. The report of the National Resources Planning Board regarding social security was clear and detailed. President Roosevelt projected a six-point plan for demobilized soldiers in his address of July 28, 1943, and shortly thereafter released a report discussing the issue. In the international field, also, some definite proposals have formed the basis of public discussion. Several have been published; the master lend-lease agreement, the draft proposals for monetary stabilization, and the Agreement for United Nations Relief and Rehabilitation Administration are familiar illustrations. The draft convention for a permanent international food and agriculture organization has been prepared; the International Labor Organization has set forth its social objectives.[1]

All these touch social and economic questions. There has been nothing equally explicit in the political field. It has been said that the peace conference in 1919 concentrated too heavily upon political considerations and failed to deal sufficiently with economic and social problems. It would be no improvement merely to reverse the error this time. The Atlantic Charter, the Four Freedoms, the Declaration by United Nations, the Moscow Declaration, and the statements at Cairo and Teheran, all of them helpful, are not so

[1] See the Philadelphia Charter of May 10, 1944. Washington, D. C. International Labor Office.

specific as the economic and social proposals. They express general principles without definite measures for their realization. Official discussion has tended to cloud, rather than clarify, their interpretation. Even if the principles had been more sharply defined, contests over their implementation might cause them to be lost. Unconditional surrender does not supply the void; it is essentially a military concept. While it opens the way for political action, it furnishes no clue regarding the line to be taken.

President Roosevelt has said: "The same kind of careful planning that gained victory in North Africa and Sicily is required if we are to make victory an enduring reality and do our share in building the kind of peaceful world which will justify the sacrifices made in this war." In harmony with that sound dictum much political planning has been done. By its nature it has been more dependent upon military events; it has also raised more sensitive issues between nations. The constructive consequences have appeared only slowly; this has led to irritating emphasis upon unfulfilled hopes, to recurrence of charges that, while policy is socially advanced, it is politically reactionary. The delay has accentuated questions regarding our relationship to the Soviet Union. It has added to the fear that though we win the war, we may lose the peace.

The public will have shortly, it is hoped, proposals on political issues [1] as explicit as the programs for social and economic reconstruction. It is not necessary, as President Roosevelt has said, to take "time out to define every boundary and settle every political controversy in every part of

---

[1] See outline of plan for post-war international security in "Statement by the President" given to the press on June 15, 1944. *N. Y. Times,* June 16, 1944, p. 1.

the world." Nor can we at this moment expect, in Prime Minister Churchill's phrase, "hard and fast conclusions or reach decisions upon all questions which torment this afflicted globe." It is needful, however, to make concrete what was first expressed only in principle. An outline of the basic terms of peace should approximate the definiteness of the Agreement for Relief and Rehabilitation Administration and the draft proposals on currency stabilization. Public discussion of tangible propositions would lead to improvements; opinion could begin to crystallize.

The suggested outline of a basic treaty does not pretend to offer a solution to all political problems. It merely explores and illustrates a possible mode of procedure in the belief that thinking will be clarified by approaching the problem concretely.

Four of the factors which determine the form and structure of such a treaty will be discussed. They are, first, the size of the problem; second, the nature of a coalition; third, the variety of American opinion; and fourth, our constitutional peculiarity, arising from the special relationship of the Senate to foreign relations. All affect both the temper and method of the proposals.

The temper is moderate; there is no effort to midwife a brave new world and no attempt to revive a world that is dead. The draft treaty seeks to clear the path to more freedom for today and to give opportunity to organize a better tomorrow. It endeavors to exploit whatever unity of thought now exists and to avoid the extremes which divide men instead of drawing them together. The method is to reduce the treaty of peace to its essentials, leaving to other treaties, agreements, or understandings whatever can best be handled by such means.

129

Before outlining the specific terms of such a treaty, two of the limiting factors need discussion—the size of the problem and the effect of a coalition war.

At the Paris Peace Conference in 1919 an effort was made to wrap as much as possible in one package. Bulky as the treaty became, it could not dispose of all the issues. Reparations, the inter-Allied debts, mandates, and many other vital matters were postponed. For nine years the Conference of Ambassadors functioned as a kind of continuing peace conference; heads of states and foreign ministers held many special supplemental conferences; and the League of Nations helped liquidate issues of the war. Actually there was a great deal of decentralization—much more than is usually thought to have been the case. Nonetheless it was not enough; the peace negotiations at Paris attempted far too much.

This was partly the consequence of underestimating the task; Mr. Lloyd George had expected that three or four weeks of inter-Allied discussions would make it possible to conclude the peace conference in a week! Partly the difficulty arose from indecision; statesmen started to frame a preliminary treaty and because of poor organization did not know when or how to stop; they went on to make a definitive treaty. Partly the wide scope was the result of design; President Wilson insisted upon including the League of Nations Covenant as an integral part of the treaty of peace. He wanted the whole pill swallowed at once, the bitter core with the sweetened coating. He hoped the Senate would accept unpalatable sections to achieve peace—much as a President sometimes signs a bill with a distasteful "rider" rather than jeopardize the whole appropriation. Whether that is ever a sound procedure may be questioned. In any event Wilson failed; the memory of that defeat is fresh and vivid in our political life. Certainly in the present temper of American politics an effort to include everything in one treaty or even one great peace conference would be incredible folly.

The proposal for a basic treaty takes account of that disastrous experience. At the end of every great war there are many treaties; in a war of the present dimensions and extended duration there will be more than ever before. By making a peace treaty of limited scope, the over-all pattern can be set; thereafter the different phases need not be crowded into one unwieldy negotiation at one time or one place.

In making peace there should be no delay for delay's sake. A general cooling-off period is a fallacious idea. Zeal often cools more rapidly than anger. Issues should be met as soon as they are ripe; some are early and urgent, others mature slowly and cannot be dealt with until they can be defined. With foresight and skill the enormously complicated questions can be broken up and dealt with piecemeal at different times and places in the order of their urgency or significance, or as they are reduced to manageable proportions. That process can begin before the war ends; indeed, it is already well under way, as the three agreements, previously referred to, indicate. There has long been insistent pressure for the crystallization of the United Nations into institutional form as a basis for a post-war world organization; evidence accumulates that the process is under way. This method, if continuously pursued, will relieve statesmen of some of the pressures which became so intolerable in 1919. It will help avoid undue strain upon the ties of alliance. It will also prevent indigestion in the body politic from swallowing too much too quickly.

Lend-lease illustrated the point. The idea was before the public a considerable time. After it had won acceptance, the master agreements were negotiated with Article VII[1] as their heart. It was not as explicit and clear-cut as desired, but in diplomatic exchanges a first formulation seldom attains that objective. In his letter of August 25, 1943, transmitting a lend-lease report[2] to Congress, President Roosevelt said: "The Congress in passing and extending the Lend-Lease Act made it plain that the United States wants no new war debts to jeopardize the coming peace. Victory

[1] Art. VII reads as follows:

In the final determination of the benefits to be provided to the United States of America by the Government of the United Kingdom in return for aid furnished under the Act of Congress of March 11, 1941, the terms and conditions thereof shall be such as not to burden commerce between the two countries, but to promote mutually advantageous economic relations between them and the betterment of world-wide economic relations. To that end, they shall include provision for agreed action by the United States of America and the United Kingdom, open to participation by all other countries of like mind, directed to the expansion, by appropriate international and domestic measures, of production, employment, and the exchange and consumption of goods, which are the material foundations of the liberty and welfare of all peoples; to the elimination of all forms of discriminatory treatment in international commerce, and to the reduction of tariffs and other trade barriers; and, in general, to the attainment of all the economic objectives set forth in the Joint Declaration made on August 12, 1941, by the President of the United States of America and the Prime Minister of the United Kingdom.

At an early convenient date, conversations shall be begun between the two Governments with a view to determining, in the light of governing economic conditions, the best means of attaining the above-stated objectives by their own agreed action and of seeking the agreed action of other like-minded Governments. (*Thirteenth Report to Congress on Lend-Lease Operations,* 78th Cong., 2d sess., House Doc. No. 375, Jan. 10, 1944.)

[2] Eleventh Quarterly Report on Lend Lease Operations.

and a secure peace are the only coin in which we can be repaid." Perhaps that was a trial balloon to test the reaction of Congress and the public to a more explicit interpretation. If so, the balloon failed to float, for the passage was soon repudiated; "There was truth in those words, the President said, but it was a condensation of the truth which might lead to misunderstanding."

The incident illustrates how democratic statesmanship must give opportunity for the crystallization of a real concensus of opinion upon one segment of the broad problem. If our government is to act wisely and firmly, it must know that the American people will support its commitments. It will move openly, never clandestinely. A democratic peace must allow time for the public to understand the central issues of a vast settlement. A basic peace treaty would establish a norm by which subsequent specific agreements could be tested.

The second limiting factor which shapes the suggested proposals arises out of the fact of coalition. Alliances are always imperfect unions. The United States learned that truth in one hard lesson, and has made no treaty of alliance since 1778. In the last war President Wilson would not even use the word; he always spoke of the United States as an associated, not an allied, power. It was a significant reservation on the part of the prophet of a united world. He entered upon the negotiations for an armistice in October 1918, without conferring with our associates in the war; they were frantic with nervousness lest he commit them before consultation. On the way to the Peace Conference, in a talk to the staff of the American Commission to Negotiate Peace, he emphasized our detachment.

There was an unconscious, but no less real, connection between that attitude and the fact that the United States ultimately made a separate treaty restoring friendly relations. If Wilson had separatist reservations, it is no wonder that others, less ardent internationalists, had more. True, our separate treaty was made after the fighting was over,[1] but there can be no doubt that our repudiation of the tripartite treaty of guaranty with Britain and France, our failure to join the League and later the Court, our absence from the Council of Ambassadors, and our disembodied presence in the capacity of unofficial observers at supplementary conferences all helped destroy the solidarity of the peace. All were foreshadowed in our refusal to make firm joint commitments as a full-fledged ally during the fighting.

Even in this war we have not yet gone the whole distance. Though President Roosevelt uses the word "allies," we have no treaty of alliance such as that between the Soviet Union and Great Britain. Our status as an ally, therefore, is distinctly limited; our commitments are more moral than legal. Though this seems a nuance to many Americans, it is clearly a matter of major concern in the minds of our allies, for it leaves the door open for separatist actions on our part.

American attention has been focused not upon our own limited liability but upon the evidences that the Soviet Union keeps to a somewhat independent course. To many the Soviets have seemed to approximate the position of an "associated" power; they are not at war with all our enemies—specifically Japan. Russia's distinctive relationship to the war was highlighted by Prime Minister Churchill, broadcasting from the Citadel in Quebec: "It would not

[1] It was signed with Germany on August 25, 1921.

134

have been suitable for Russia to be represented at this Anglo-American conference, which . . . was largely . . . concerned with heating and inflaming the war against Japan, with whom the Soviet Government has a five-years' treaty of non-aggression; it would have been an embarrassing invitation for us to send." It is no use to insist that this is fully "one war" under such circumstances; we only deceive ourselves in so doing. A war of coalition is seldom "one war." As fighting proceeds it sometimes becomes more nearly, and at other times less nearly, one war.

Separatism, of whatever degree, arises from lack of identity of interests. The differences between the Soviet Union and ourselves should be recognized, and neither exaggerated nor minimized. The divergence in point of view is old, and it runs deep; it cannot be cured by a verbal formula. To bridge it will require time, patience, and wise statesmanship, for it stems from lack of confidence—on both sides. For our part, we have feared communism; we long refused recognition to the Soviets; our confidence was alienated by the failure of the Comintern to live up to the agreements of the Government—Tweedledee insisted he was not Tweedledum. Again Winston Churchill's extraordinary candor stated the point. When the Soviet Union entered the war he accepted the new ally, but said explicitly that he withdrew none of his earlier criticism. For his part, Stalin intimated that Britain and France would gladly have embroiled Germany with Russia to escape war in the West; that was one reason for his fateful pact with Hitler in 1939. He did not open Pandora's box, but by that treaty he gave the Nazis leave to do so—with the classic result. When it is assumed (as it has been stylish to do) that Stalin has always been correct in his realistic judgments, this error should not be forgotten.

While Stalin was insistently calling for a second front, Churchill did not resent his "complaints and even reproaches." Nevertheless the British Prime Minister recalled that "we once had a fine front in France, but it was torn to pieces . . . and it is easier to have a front pulled down than it is to build it up again." He did not need to remind Stalin that during that tragic debacle, the Soviet Union was despoiling Poland, the Baltic States, and Finland. It was no thanks to Stalin that Britain stood firm; he was fortunate that there was any springboard from which to launch an attack on Hitler from the West.

The United States had a very engrossing second front in the Pacific and the Far East. It constituted an assignment so arduous as seriously to impair our capacity to establish a new front in western Europe as speedily as Stalin desired. Meanwhile it protected the Soviets from having to fight on a second front. But this ally avoided our urgent second front so sedulously that when American aviators were forced to land on Soviet territory they were interned, and could not even fight the common enemy, Hitler.

We have fought another costly battle on the Atlantic, against the submarine. From that war also this ally is absent, though victory in that sector is essential to the flow of lend-lease materials to the Soviet Union. It is also vital to the establishment of the particular second front Stalin demanded. Prime Minister Churchill suggested that the leader of the land-fighting Russians did not fully appreciate the problems of amphibious warfare.

A second front in Italy was heavily depreciated by Russia until the Italians surrendered. That front, however, shook the political structure of the Axis to its foundations. In masses of troops it did not compare with the Russian front; communications and supply problems made that impossible. Nonetheless its political effect has been immense. Italy became an enemy to Hitler, whose Balkan allies also started groping for peace.

These things are recalled solely to emphasize that mutual trust and confidence cannot be attained by wishful thinking. Stalin is said to be a realist; it is no flattery to a realist to grow sentimental about him. Yet that has been the tone of much recent discussion. So far as we know them, several desires of the Soviet Union run counter to ours. Stalin apparently wants all the Baltic States, a sizable part of Poland, and territory in the Balkans. His policy touching Germany also contrasts with ours—he speaks plainly of leaving Germany partly armed; he does not look forward to complete unilateral disarmament. European federations, desired by some of the United Nations, were denounced in a Soviet organ, and particularly any federation of eastern Europe which might appear to be "leveled against the Soviet Union." Russia's old fear of a *cordon sanitaire* dies hard.

These and other divergencies of view must be taken into account. There are hopeful signs that in working together for victory old suspicions have been allayed; experience of common action has bred confidence. There is need for continued progress. The Soviet Union will come to the end of the war with incomparably the biggest army in Europe. It may be flushed with triumph and a sense of having been the major factor in producing victory. It will not necessarily have a Japanese war to liquidate; presumably we shall still have that difficult problem. It will no longer need our lend-lease supplies; our leverage will be declining while Russia's bargaining position grows apace. It may be at its zenith when a peace conference assembles.

The Soviet Union is of vital importance to us in this war; we are of vital importance to Soviet victory. We ought to continue in full collaboration to win the war; we should also work together to maintain the peace. But to expect history suddenly to be rolled back is absurd; to hope that differences so old and so profound can be wholly resolved in a short time is simply to fly in the face of reality.

We should make up our minds, therefore, to draft the kind of peace that both can sign without reservations; it should minimize and mitigate the differences. We should exploit what Secretary Hull called the "areas of common interest"; then we must trust to time and skill for the solution of problems not yet capable of being mastered. Such a program would leave to separate settlement whatever can safely be left to that process. To some extent that procedure would dissipate the immediate collisions of policy, whereas to concentrate them into sharp focus at a general peace conference might destroy the peace.

The position of the Soviet Union dramatizes some of the influences of a coalition war upon the structure of a peace treaty. But its particular problems are by no means the only ones. A coalition war and a coalition peace involve uneven participation in the war and unequal interest in various aspects of the peace. This is one world, and a great nation like the United States has interests which touch every region on earth. But while there is a universality of interest, it is of greatly varying intensity.

Pan Americanism, recognized even by its critics as "one of the immutable principles of the foreign policy of the

United States," is based on the assumption that no European power can have interests in this hemisphere either so extensive or so intensive as our own. That being so, we must accept the corollaries—that the Soviet Union has a deeper stake in eastern Europe than we, China a livelier concern with the western Pacific, and Australia with the southern Pacific. Any other assumption is arrogant, however unconscious, imperialism. The peace treaty must not commit us greatly beyond our "fundamental national interest"—nor can we expect to exercise an influence substantially greater than our stake. This strongly suggests that the treaty should be a kind of greatest common denominator; it cannot cover all problems.

Local issues should be largely excluded and, within the framework of general principles, left to local settlement. That is the real significance of regionalism. As a formula, regionalism has been badly overdone because it has been too closely identified with institutions. But if we look at it less formally and institutionally it makes good sense. There has been far too much tendency to talk as though a new world could be put together by the President and the Prime Minister, or by a "Big Three," or a "Big Four." That will never do. If we are to achieve a peaceful world, the smaller countries must have a vital part.

Because military might plays so dominant a role in war, we tend now to think of power as a peace-time measure of the importance of a nation. Some current discussion tends to wave small powers aside with a cavalier gesture. We should remember that it was not they who fled from responsible action or defaulted their international obligations between the two wars. And in this war itself, the moral and physical courage of the Norwegians, the Dutch, the Greeks, the Yugoslavs, and others should not be discounted in assessing the ingredients of victory. The strength and wisdom of small nations are not measured by their military might. If, as Secretary Hull said, the small sovereignties are "in law and under law the equal of every other nation," they are properly jealous of their rights. The suggested plan lets them deal with the matters which concern them most deeply.

There is a dispute between the Netherlands and Belgium with regard to the Scheldt; it is important that it should be settled. The precise nature of that settlement, however, is of no profound significance to us, and those who can best arrange it are the Netherlands and Belgium. A boundary dispute between Czechoslovakia and Poland can be a threat to the peace of the world, but the line will be better drawn if they determine it and if we do not underwrite it. They know that any such guaranty would become sterile in the course of time, just as our underwriting of the prohibition upon German militarization of the Rhineland became meaningless. In many of these regional disputes, moreover, states now neutral have lively interests. Sweden, Turkey, and Switzerland cannot be neglected, but they should not be drawn into questions from which their neutrality properly excludes them.

The ultimate substance of regionalism is not a mass of formal federations such as the Soviet Union has denounced. It is the steady and continuous resolution of local differences by the powers immediately concerned, upon bases which the nations less intimately involved can approve and recognize. This means that there may be many treaties in the negotiation of which the United States might play a useful part as friend and counsellor, without becoming a signatory, because formal participation would certainly lead to needless domestic difficulties. Moreover signing such treaties might put us falsely in the position of a major partner, where our interests are really minor. That would eventually mean instability. Our good offices are more valuable than our bargaining power in situations in which our concern is not direct.

Dividing up the task of settlement is more realistic in still another way. The solutions of various problems should not all pretend to equal finality. There must be room for many changes. If there is not free opportunity for orderly change, then changes will surely be made by force. When too many questions are rolled into one vast treaty structure, it tends to lend equal finality to all solutions. Then any small break imperils the whole fabric—as each violation of the Versailles system weakened the entire structure.

Two limiting factors—the dimensions of the problem and the fact of coalition—have been discussed. The other two—domestic opinion and the Senate's powers—can best be considered after examining the draft treaty.

The proposal involves a separate treaty between each of the Axis powers upon the one hand and all the United Nations at war with it upon the other. That is not a novel idea; in fact it was the procedure followed at the Paris Conference. While we usually speak of the Versailles Treaty as ending the World War, it dealt only with Germany. Austria's treaty was signed at St. Germain, Hungary's at the Trianon, Bulgaria's at Neuilly, and Turkey's at Sèvres and later at Lausanne. This proposal, therefore, differs in scope rather than basic procedure.

Each peace treaty should resolve the major issues between all the United Nations and one of the defeated powers. It should settle matters in outline rather than detail, leaving time and circumstance, patience and skill to work out the particulars. It would be a dictated peace; the United Nations would negotiate it among themselves, and the treaty would be presented to the enemy as the terms of peace. It should provide as harsh treatment as the enemy is ever to receive, allowing for subsequent mitigation if and when it becomes justified—as a prison term may be shortened by good behavior.

On one point of procedure it should follow exactly the opposite pattern from 1919. President Wilson refused to make an armistice, much less sign a treaty, with the Kaiser's government. He insisted upon revolution as a prerequisite. The effect was to put the humiliation of a hard peace upon the successor government, not the perpetrators of war. This treaty should bear the signature of Adolph Hitler and the Chief of the German General Staff. Let the authors of the war admit defeat. Revolution will occur; no need to worry about that. But if at all possible, let the successor government escape the whole opprobrium of surrender.

Each treaty should be brief enough and so clearly expressed that every citizen can read and understand it. Such was the draft in preparation for Secretary of State Lansing before the Paris Conference; such, also, was the Treaty of Brest-Litovsk by which Germany made peace with the Bolsheviks in 1918. In preparing this draft the arbitrary assumption was made that it should not be longer than the Constitution of the United States. The outline might be as follows:

ARTICLE I. *Peace is restored.*

This clause has sweeping legal effects in both domestic and international law. It is modeled upon the Treaty of

142

Bucharest of 1896—a classic of brevity, for this was its only provision; all other matters at issue were settled through unilateral action by each of the powers involved.

ARTICLE II. *Germany shall evacuate all occupied territory and demobilize all armed forces; all warships, all airplanes, all war matériel shall be immediately surrendered to the United Nations. All waters controlled by Germany shall promptly be cleared of every hostile device, and all defensive works on land destroyed. The whole operation shall be under the supervision of the United Nations, which may occupy part or all of Germany for such time as may seem to them desirable.*

This is as near unconditional surrender as it is possible to get. It fulfills the eighth provision of the Atlantic Charter: "Since no future peace can be maintained if land, sea, or air armaments continue to be employed by nations which threaten, or may threaten, aggression outside of their frontiers, . . . pending the establishment of a wider and permanent system of general security, . . . the disarmament of such nations is essential." Complete unilateral disarmament of the enemy, moreover, contains no inferential promise of any like action on our part, such as bedeviled the Versailles Treaty.

ARTICLE III. *The boundaries of Germany shall be those of January 30, 1933.*

That cancels every Hitlerite gain. It resists a natural temptation to dismember Germany. There can be no question that many plans for reducing the size of Germany have been considered—lopping off the Rhineland, taking away the Saar, giving East Prussia to Poland, and so on. Some appear to have strong official support. Speaking on May 23, 1944, the British Prime Minister said:

"The essential part of any arrangement is the regulation of the Polish eastern frontier, and in return for any withdrawals made by Poland in that quarter she should receive other territories at the expense of Germany which will give her an ample seaboard and a good, adequate and reasonable homeland in which the Polish nation can safely dwell." "The Atlantic Charter in no way binds us about the future of Germany. . . . There is no question of Germany enjoying any guarantee of any kind that she shall not undergo territorial changes, if it should seem that making such changes would render more secure and more lasting the peace of Europe."

Despite such distinguished sponsorship, it remains doubtful that the problem of the Soviet-Polish boundary can be "solved" by creating a new and perhaps more difficult issue.

If the integrity of Germany is respected, it would not be through tenderness to Germany, but because new irredentisms lay foundations for future war. We want no more Alsace-Lorraines. We do well to remember that after Poland had thrice been partitioned and was "abolished" for over a century, it still lived on. We should not now attempt what history has shown to be impossible.

Moreover, to take away territory from one nation as "punishment," or to add it to another as "reward" or "compensation," gives the color of support to the right of conquest, the abolition of which is vital to the peace of the world. To parcel out conquests also looks like contravention of the self-denying promise of the Atlantic Charter to "seek no aggrandizement, territorial or other." The peace should have no tincture of bad faith; the Atlantic Charter should be scrupulously—even meticulously—respected if at all possible.

This proposal is based on one other fundamental assumption—that the best boundary is a fixed boundary. As

Colonel House said after weary experience, "To create new boundaries is to create new troubles." A completely satisfactory boundary is a rarity; there are very few in all the world that cannot be challenged upon some basis— strategic, geographic, economic, linguistic, ethnographic, or cultural. Most can be criticized on several grounds. Despite enormous difficulties, it is usually easier to adjust other factors to existing boundaries than to alter established lines. Stability is their most important quality.

ARTICLE IV. *All colonies and mandates shall be transferred to the United Nations, who will determine their future status.*

This clause has no relevance in the case of Germany since it has neither colonies nor mandates. It is inserted as a model for use in treaties with Italy and Japan. There is no single, simple, over-all solution to the colonial problem; this allows greatest flexibility in final decisions.

ARTICLE V. *Germany agrees that all its treaties, laws, regulations, port dues, tariffs, inspection methods, charges of every kind, and foreign exchange controls shall, as to the rest of the world, be uniform and equal, without any discrimination, difference, or preference, direct or indirect.*

Germany shall immediately reveal all existing treaties, agreements, and understandings; any inconsistent with the first paragraph of this Article shall become inoperative forthwith. All future treaties, agreements, and understandings are to be made public immediately.

This provision is based to some extent upon a draft article prepared twenty-five years ago for Secretary Lansing. It is calculated to implement, on the part of Germany, the fifth principle of the Atlantic Charter: "To bring about the fullest collaboration between all nations in the economic field with the object of securing, for all, improved labor standards, economic advancement and social security." And it is designed to harmonize German policy with the temper of Article VII of the master lend-lease agreement. The purpose is to put an end to the kind of ruthless economic imperialism which gave Hitler some of his cheapest victories.

ARTICLE VI. *Germany shall restore all tangible property, of whatever sort, to its rightful owners.*

All merchant ships shall be delivered to the United Nations for immediate use, without compensation to Germany, in the distribution of food, clothing, medical and other supplies to the inhabitants of the territories occupied by Germany and to such others as the United Nations may determine. The ships may subsequently be delivered to nations in compensation for shipping destroyed by Germany, or they may be returned to Germany at the discretion of the United Nations.

Germany shall deliver to the Bank for International Settlements, as trustee for the United Nations, all publicly or privately held evidences of ownership or of debt of all properties located outside the Reich as it existed on the thirtieth day of January, 1933; any compensation to its citizens shall be at the expense of Germany.

Germany shall also deliver to the Bank for International Settlements, as trustee for the United Nations, clear title, free of debt, to all properties within the Reich, any part of which was owned on September 1, 1939, by persons of other than German nationality.

Reparations are a bugaboo. One would think that after the last experience no temptation to excess would remain. Yet the demand for reparations is rising in many countries.

These provisions are designed to get what can be gotten promptly, to acquire the German patents in the hands of Swiss holding companies, and to recover what has been stolen or bought with printing-press money.

ARTICLE VII. *Germany agrees to cease and refrain from all agitation and propaganda against the governments or the public institutions of other countries.*

Germany agrees to provide freedom of access to news and its unhampered exchange domestically and internationally.

The first paragraph of this Article is based upon the Treaty of Brest-Litovsk forced upon Russia by Germany in 1918. The second is designed for the enlightenment of the German people through one of the Four Freedoms.

ARTICLE VIII. *Germany shall release all prisoners of war and pay all costs of their return to their homes.*

ARTICLE IX. *Germany agrees to an immediate and definitive end to every kind of personal discrimination against Jews, other minorities, and foreign workers. All persons under restraint, detained, or imprisoned for political reasons shall be released and assisted to re-establish themselves. Foreign workers shall be free of all compulsion and each permitted to settle in the country of his choice, at the cost of Germany.*

ARTICLE X. *Germany accepts responsibility for the repatriation, at its own expense, of all German nationals dwelling outside the Reich who desire to be repatriated, or who are expelled by any signatory power.*

Germany also agrees to the principle and practice of the exchange of populations under United Nations direction, all the costs to be borne by Germany.

This is the most drastic provision in the draft treaty, but

147

it is the least radical solution of a crucial issue. The Paris Peace Conference gave Europe the best set of boundaries it ever had, but no boundary can prevent minorities, and treaties for the protection of minorities notably failed. An exchange of minorities achieves the purpose. At the end of the last war plebiscites to determine boundaries made infinite trouble. The exchange of Greeks and Turks, on the other hand, produced a satisfactory solution. Admittedly this is hard on those who are moved—but neither so hard on them nor the rest of the world as periodic wars.

The suggested exchange of population is a large order. It would mean moving at least five million persons. Before we set that down as hopelessly large, let us bring it into perspective. Early in the twentieth century as many as two million persons emigrated from Europe each year, at their own expense and without government assistance. Within the United States there was an annual shift of population of very large proportions. The Germans, during the present war, have transferred or colonized perhaps three million people. The problem, therefore, while serious, is not insoluble.

Of all times in history this is the most favorable moment. Enormous numbers of persons in the regions most vitally affected have been dispossessed by the ravages of war. The present dislocation of population through mobilization, labor migration, military occupation, and population transfers runs to well over one hundred million people. The proposed exchange would involve a number only five per cent as large. Drastic as this solution seems at first sight, in the long view it is probably the least costly and the most humane.

ARTICLE XI. *Germany shall deliver to the United Na-*

tions for trial and punishment, under procedures to be established by the United Nations, all Germans accused of violence or crimes committed during the war in violation of law or human rights.

To this we are fully committed.[1] Perhaps we should remind ourselves that Articles 228, 229, and 230 of the Versailles Treaty provided much the same thing; a list of nearly a thousand was drawn up, a few were tried, some were convicted and then escaped. The Kaiser was to be hung—but the Netherlands granted him asylum. We have warned neutrals against furnishing places of refuge; so far their reception of the admonition has not been favorable.

ARTICLE XII. *Pending a definitive agreement between the United Nations and Germany, full authority to issue and to take all measures to control the currency of Germany is vested in an Economic Commission to be appointed by the United Nations.*

The purpose of this is to establish such controls as may be necessary to prevent a runaway inflation.

ARTICLE XIII. *Germany agrees, if invited, to participate in regional or world organizations which may hereafter be established, upon such terms and conditions as may be defined by the United Nations at any time within a period of five years.*

This secures Germany's adherence, if desired, to any future organization; it does not commit the United Nations —or any of them—to any specific international organization. After the experience of the last war no proposal to include

---

[1] President Roosevelt made this clear in his statement of October 7, 1942, announcing American participation in the United Nations Commission for the Investigation of War Crimes. (Department of State, *Bulletin*, VII, p. 797.)

a new association of nations within the treaty could possibly succeed. Public opinion is only slowly crystallizing as to what kind of organization is desirable. The address of Secretary Hull on September 12, 1943, gave clear evidence of that fact; he said the problem was being "studied intensively," and "gradually" being made the subject "of consultation between and among governments." The Declaration of Moscow, the adoption of resolutions by the Senate and House of Representatives were further indications of progress. By the spring of 1944 the Prime Minister and the President were more explicit, conversations are now in progress to give form and substance to the United Nations idea. We seem to be moving empirically through alliance and the United Nations framework. Conceivably, indeed preferably, the basic organization might be established before the peace conference.

ARTICLE XIV. *Agreements among the United Nations shall implement this treaty.*

ARTICLE XV. *Upon ratification of this treaty, an armistice shall be effective in each theater of war as proclaimed by the Commander of the United Nations forces.*

The last two articles open up the whole question of the constitutional position of the Senate. It will be observed that there is no armistice, no cessation of fighting until the treaty is ratified. That is not a trick; it is designed to cure one of the great evils of American foreign relations, and it is based upon sound historical precedent.

Nothing so inhibits our negotiators, nothing leads other nations to be so reluctant to make commitments with the United States as the fear that the Senate will not consent to ratification. Clemenceau yielded many points in exchange for the tripartite treaty of guaranty. When the

Senate repudiated that, he had made his concessions without compensation. He lost the presidency of France, and retired in bitterness.

Historically, treaties of peace have had especially hard sledding. The Treaty of Guadalupe-Hidalgo which concluded the war with Mexico had a rough passage in the Senate during a period of fifteen days. Three articles were eliminated and two others were altered. A number of amendments were considered and ultimately rejected. Only after this were advice and consent to ratification obtained.

When the treaty of peace at the end of the Spanish-American War was laid before the Senate it became the subject of debate for over a month and was approved with only two votes to spare. Senator Lodge said while it was under consideration: "I cannot think calmly of the rejection of this Treaty by a little more than one-third of the Senate. It would be a repudiation of the President and humiliation of the country in the eyes of the whole world, and would show we are unfit as a nation to enter into great questions of foreign policy." When the fight was over, he exclaimed: "It was the closest, hardest fight I have ever known, and probably we shall not see another in our time in which there was so much at stake."

The world has special reason to be hesitant now, for since the Washington Conference of 1922 no treaty of large political importance has come before the Senate. Despite the difficulties, we do not want to evade the Constitution. Doubtless most American citizens would be glad to see the Constitution amended to provide for ratification of a treaty by a simple majority in both houses of Congress. But the likelihood that such an amendment could be adopted in war-time is slender. It would be so obvious an abdication of function that the Senate would probably lack the political courage to yield such powers even if most senators thought it wise—and that is questionable.

There is, however, one kind of treaty the Senate would presumably accept. Article I of the separate treaty with Germany at the end of the last war stated: "The United States shall have and enjoy, all the rights, privileges, indemnities, reparations or advantages . . . stipulated for the benefit of the United States in the Treaty of Versailles . . . notwithstanding the fact that such a Treaty has not been ratified by the United States." When Senator Lodge, as Chairman of the Foreign Relations Committee, introduced the treaty, he said, "We secure every advantage. . . . We are left absolutely free in regard to assuming any obligations."

In a like manner the suggested draft treaty is unilateral in its obligations; it lays burdens upon the enemy, it confers powers upon us, but makes no heavy commitments for the future. Personally I should like to see us agree to accept responsibilities correlative with our position of power; however, this draft does not represent my idea of the best kind of peace; it is an exploration of method. It attempts to achieve some ends which are almost undebatable. We shall have to seek other desirable ends by a harder process. The treaty would clear the decks.

The present draft provides that the political settlement should precede the armistice. Far from being a novel proposal, that is actually the normal procedure. Many times in our history the political settlement has been made before fighting stopped. At the end of the Revolution the preliminary treaty was negotiated before an armistice; in the wars with the Barbary States treaties were regularly framed during hostilities; at the close of the War of 1812 the definitive treaty was ratified before fighting ceased; in the Mexican War the general in command was instructed to proclaim an armistice only after Mexico had ratified the treaty; in the Spanish-American War the bases of peace were set out in a protocol before an armistice, and in the World War by an exchange of notes. All sought the same objective; the means varied only in procedural detail. This treaty simply follows the basic idea of all those precedents, and selects the most appropriate and successful among those methods.

The specific provision that there be no armistice until ratification is based upon unimpeachable American historical practice. When peace negotiations were undertaken during the War of 1812, a first draft of Article I of the Treaty of Ghent provided that "all hostilities, both by sea and land, shall immediately cease." But the British commissioners, aware of the Senate's functions, inserted the words "after the exchange of ratifications." In its final form, the Article read: "All hostilities, both by sea and land, shall cease as soon as this treaty shall have been ratified by both parties." The treaty reached Washington late in the evening of February 14, 1815, and was considered at a Cabinet meeting that same night. The next day, in a message to the Senate, President Madison said: "The termination of hostilities depends upon the time of the ratification of the treaty by both parties. I lose no time, therefore, in submitting the treaty to the Senate for their advice and approbation." The Senate read the treaty, reviewed the instructions of the envoys at Ghent and examined their correspondence with the Department of State, and then voted advice and con-

153

sent to ratification unanimously on February 16. The following day, ratifications were duly exchanged.

Here was an instance where the power of a minority indefinitely to obstruct was fairly checkmated, without any attempt to by-pass the Constitution. The treaty was of such dimensions that it could be quickly read and easily understood. Lengthy debate meant needlessly prolonging the fighting; the procedure provided both fair consideration and promptitude.

It is a sound historical precedent. In that instance we were giving assurance to our enemy that cessation of fighting really meant peace. In this instance we should be giving assurance to our allies that they are not asked to agree to something, to make concessions to our desire, only to have the whole business repudiated. The world must gain confidence that we will support our commitments—not momentarily, but steadily and faithfully. One European statesman, very popular in America, asked bluntly, "Are you going to leave another baby on our doorstep and run away again?"

There is every reason to believe senators will agree that the proposed procedure is fair. Though it seems evident that the Senate will not yield its right to advise and consent to ratification, it clearly does not want again to take the responsibility for destroying the structure of peace by a minority vote. Nor does the Senate want to accept responsibility for delay so protracted as to be even worse than killing the treaty outright.

Having freely and fully recognized the right of the Senate, we may give attention to Article XIV which provides implementation by agreements. This also is based upon unimpeachable precedent and established practice.

The employment of executive agreements is almost as old as the Government of the United States. Often their subject matter has been indistinguishable from treaties. In at least one class of agreements they were first regarded as treaties and subsequently, without protest on the part of anyone, as executive agreements. In some instances they have even been called "treaties"—postal treaties, for example—though they were executive agreements. One executive agreement was approved by a two-thirds vote of the Senate, though it was not a treaty. Another executive agreement is printed in the official Treaty Series of the Department of State. In one instance the same instrument is regarded as an agreement by the United States and as a treaty by the other party. No one—neither the Supreme Court, nor Congress, nor the Executive—has ever drawn a sharp, clear, differentiating definition which puts executive agreements on one side and treaties on the other. From the standpoint of a lexicographer this may appear to be confusion; in the art of government we call it flexibility.

The bases upon which executive agreements have been predicated are varied. Many have grown out of presidential control of foreign relations. Sometimes these agreements have had inferential Congressional approval by subsequent appropriations to effectuate them. Executive agreements have also been founded upon statutes and joint resolutions of Congress. As the Supreme Court said in a notable decision: [1]

"Practically every volume of the United States Statutes contains one or more acts or joint resolutions of Congress authorizing action by the President in respect of subjects affecting

[1] *United States* v. *Curtiss-Wright Export Corporation*, 1936, 299 U. S. 304.

foreign relations, which either leave the exercise of the power to his unrestricted judgment, or provide a standard far more general than that which has always been considered requisite with regard to domestic affairs."

As early as 1912 the Supreme Court held that an executive agreement,[1] even though no ratification was voted by the Senate, "was an international compact, negotiated between the representatives of two sovereign nations and made in the name and on behalf of the contracting countries. . . . If not technically a treaty requiring ratification, nevertheless it was a compact authorized by the Congress of the United States, negotiated and proclaimed under the authority of its President."

Executive agreements have also been based upon the authority of a treaty—as in this proposal. A whole series of such agreements, extending from 1916 to 1934, implemented a treaty with Haiti made in 1915; the treaty authorized agreements "with the President of the United States." That instance is by no means unique.

In settling a war of the present dimensions we shall need all the flexibility our constitutional procedure allows. The proposal to supplement the peace treaty by agreements involves no strain upon the Constitution. It merely employs an old instrument firmly established in our constitutional practice.

The prerequisite for its effective utilization is a spirit of mutual confidence. We seem on the way to achieve that. Fear was expressed in Congress that the Senate was to be by-passed. It was suggested that an effort might be made to diffuse the settlement, and, in effect, to conceal it in such a vast number of specific agreements, understandings, com-

[1] *United States* v. *Altman & Co.*, 1912, 224 U. S. 583.

156

mitments, legislative resolutions, laws, and treaties that the total pattern would not be clear. The peace might, so to speak, be "put over" on Congress and the people.

The publication of the draft agreement regarding United Nations Relief and Rehabilitation Administration brought the matter to an open issue. It produced a vigorous passage at arms between the Chairman of the Senate Foreign Relations Committee and the Secretary of State who had asserted that "participation in the establishment of this United Nations administration should be through an executive agreement." The stage was set for a constitutional struggle between the Senate and the Executive. To avoid a direct clash there were conversations between a subcommittee of the Foreign Relations Committee and officers of the State Department.

Let us ardently hope that at least a preliminary treaty of peace will be made between the two ends of Pennsylvania Avenue. Sometimes when the clamor was loudest for the President to keep on going to the ends of the earth to meet with Joseph Stalin and other foreign statesmen, it seemed even more desirable that he should arrange a conference with Tom Connally. Secretary Hull has done much to bring harmony.

At all events there is reason to believe that the Senate will be content if it is given an unequivocal opportunity to act upon the formal treaty of peace, and will view with relief the prospect of that treaty being implemented, supplemented, and realized by legislation and by executive agreements authorized by the treaty itself or approved by appropriations or by other legislative action. The Senate has no desire to be merely an instrument of obstruction.

It is good to have this issue thrashed out now and the

atmosphere cleared. No one can seriously believe there was ever any intention to "put over" a peace settlement. It would be a self-defeating maneuver. If a series of diplomatic tricks could achieve a kind of *fait accompli*, such a jerry-built arrangement would go to pieces in short order. Both our allies and our enemies would recognize its furtive techniques and would know that the process was inherently unstable. Public opinion here at home would repudiate it overwhelmingly.

The fourth factor, the variety of American opinion, can be disposed of in a few words. This draft treaty was drawn in the consciousness that a national election is approaching. The treaty may be negotiated in the midst of a political campaign. It may be framed by one party and carried out by another. The minority when it is signed will, under the pendulum action of politics, almost inevitably be the majority at some later time. If ever there was a moment to heed the aphorism, "politics should stop at the water's edge," this is the moment. As Secretary Hull expressed it: "The supreme importance of these problems should lift them far above the realm of partisan considerations or party politics." Everything should be done to unite us, nothing needlessly to divide. This draft commits us neither to the international sentimentalists with their dreams of milk and honey nor to the hard-shell isolationists with their blind prejudices. It leaves the way open for public opinion to mature step by step.

To summarize: such a treaty reveals the political implications of unconditional surrender; it makes separate treaties with each enemy as it is detached from the Axis; it removes the blockade and allows the prompt feeding of the populace; it excludes the enemy from discussion of inter-Allied

problems; it leaves to bilateral or group settlement problems
of limited scope; it gives time for the slower, piecemeal
solution of numerous problems. Domestically it can be
supported by persons of many shades of political opinion; it
makes possible assent of the Senate at the most favorable
moment; it provides for implementation of the treaty with
the most flexible of all our diplomatic instruments, without
depriving Congress of its check upon the Executive.